THE LONDON BOOK CO
3-KOHSAR MARKET, F-6/3
ISLAMABAD - PAKISTAN
PH # 823852 FAX # 201838

Human Records
on
Karakorum Highway

Human Records on Karakorum Highway

Prof. Ahmad Hasan Dani
Professor Emeritus
Quaid-e-Azam University

SANG-E-MEEL PUBLICATIONS
25, Shahrah-e-Pakistan (Lower Mall) Lahore

1995

© Dr. Ahmad Hasan Dani

Published by
Niaz Ahmad
Sang-e-Meel Publications
Lahore

Designed by
Ayaz Ali

Composed by
Wizards, Lahore

Printed by
Combine Printers
Lahore

Copies 1000

CONTENTS

		Page
	Preface	7
1.	Mountain Terrian	9
2.	Silk Road	11
3.	Chinese Pilgrim Route	13
4.	Journey Through Karakorum Highway	22
5.	Rock Edicts of Mansehra	23
6.	Hazara Plain to the Indus	25
7.	Kohistan	28
8.	Shatial and Darel Valley	29
9.	From Shatial to Thor	32
10.	Hodur	34
11.	From Hodur to Chilas	35
12.	Chilas	45
13.	Chilas II	50
14.	Gondophares Rock	59
15.	Chilas I	60
16.	Thalpan Plain	65
17.	From Chilas to Gilgit	73
18.	Gilgit	77
19.	From Gilgit to Hunza	83
20.	Sacred Rock of Hunza	84
21.	From Hunza to Khunjrab	101

Chilas II. Man standing on horse with bow and arrow

PREFACE

SECOND EDITION

As the first edition of the book was finished long ago this second edition is being published on an entirely new format and with new material added to the original text. The discovery of gold waist-band from Pattan in Kohistan has been a unique find in Pakistan and speaks of the movement of the Scythians on this route. At the same time the decipherment of the inscriptions at the Sacred Rock of Hunza throws light on the history of the Trakhan dynasty which succeeded the Patola-Shahis in Gilgit. The decipherment of the Chinese inscription from the same rock evidences the coming of a Chinese envoy to this region.

This new edition has been possible because of the great effort made by Mr. Niaz Ahmad of Sang-e-Meel Publications, Lahore. I hope the edition with coloured photographs will be appreciated by the readers.

Taj Mughal Stupa

Mountain Terrain (Map No. 1)

Karakorum Highway has been cut through high mountain ranges of Himalaya and Karakorum to connect Pakistan with China. It has opened a passage through isolated hilly regions that had remained a cultural backwater of humanity for millennia. The building of the Highway should be regarded as the eighth wonder of the world, wrought by cooperation of the engineers from Pakistan and China. Many of them died while blasting the rocks only to facilitate human movement and communion. The Highway itself is the greatest memorial to these martyrs to whom humanity owes a deep debt of gratitude. Their success has opened a new chapter in world's history when this road will be used by generations after generations of man not only to learn about these mountain people but also to draw together, in a common pursuit of peaceful trade, large concentration of human population as it was once done with great difficulty by the famous Silk Road.

Karakorum, literally meaning "Black Mountain", is one of the many chains that curve away from the nodal point at Pamir knot. The great Himalaya, that throws series of ranges, swerves south-east from that point and stands like a wall between the climate, flora and fauna of Chinese north and those of the sub-continental south. The Hindukush turns southwest and acts like a great barrier against the movement of people from trans-Oxus region to the Indus plain. The Ghissar and Alai mountains run almost north-south and make the line of communication between east and west difficult. To the north-east run several ranges, the most famous being Kun lun, T'ien Shan and Altai, that enclose between them the Tarim basin on the south and Dzungaria basin on the north. The entire zone inclines south-west of Mongolia and much of it has been a part of Turkestan of old. It is this terrain that was crossed by the Buddhist missionaries from Gandhara to China, Mongolia, Korea and Japan.

Beyond Himalaya monsoon ceases and life in the trans-Himalayan belt presents a picture of high altitude abode, apparently cut away from the main run of human history and locked in the isolation of hilly environment. Mountain slopes and high plateaus hold soil for forest growth, grassy pastures and man's toil to win a living out of leveled fields that range in terraces from the summit to

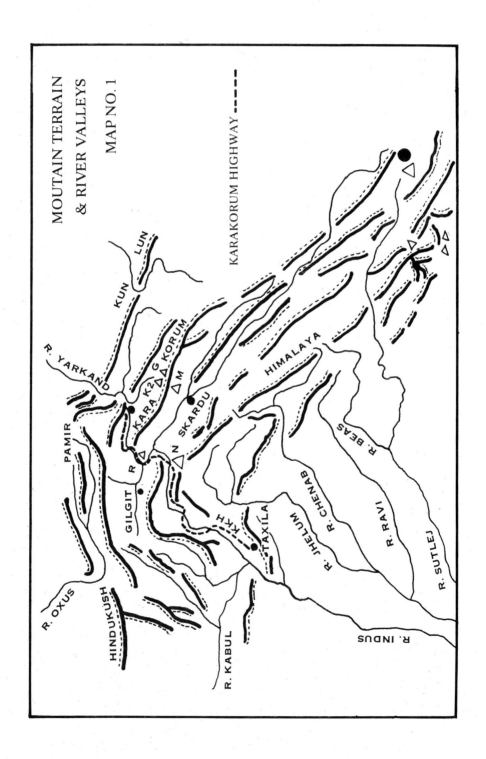

the bottom of narrow hill valleys. Living is the gift of glaciers and the melting of their snow release channels of water to quench the thirst of man and of the soil. Glacier, greenery and habitations of men intervene between bare rocks and continue the story of the earth, to be heard in the splashing water of hill torrents and in the gushing currents of the Indus and its affluents. Between Himalaya and Karakorum the mighty Indus thunders and breaks through several deep gorges, tunnels round the Nanga Parbart (Dyamar), the western-most peak of the Himalaya, and skirts the Hindukush southward towards the plain of Punjab. Human vision sees fairies and demons perched on high glaciers over the Karakorum range and on many others that follow on to Kun lun and hence the much-talked of "hanging pass" beyond Shimshal. The two basins of Tarim and Dzungaria are almost dry, desertlike, the actual desert of Taklamakan Iying to the south and that of Gobi to the far northeast. Several streams traverse the basins: Khotan, Yarkand, Tashkurgan and Kashgar lead on to Tarim, make human living possible and open channels of communication. A number of oases has concentrated human population and sustained oasis states in the dry basins. Such states have been the envies of larger states on the Hoang-ho in northern China, on the Oxus in the heart of Asia and on the Indo-Gangetic plain to the south. It is the smaller states that control the means of communication but bigger states have had great stake in transporting their goods through them. And thus the caravan has marched through history for men to contend, clash and compromise for a common human goal.

Silk Road (Map No. 2)

It is this historic relationship of the past that has given importance to this vast zone and roped it to the history of human civilization. While Hsiung-nu people, located about Dzungaria, have cast their eyes on Tarim, it is the great Han empire of China that extended its influence towards this part and controlled roads leading through it. One important item of trade, in which China was interested, was the export of Chinese silk and hence the popularity of the name— the Silk Road of old, which traversed the Tarim basin in its westward extension through Central Asia to meet the markets in the Mediterranean coast. From second century BC to about fifth century A.D the trade continued to flow. Thereafter the rise of the Hsiung-nu dislocated trade connection and the name of Silk Road survived in legendary tales.

The Silk Road started at Ch'angan (modern Si-gan-fu, or Xian former capital of the province of Shen-si) on the north-western borders of China and

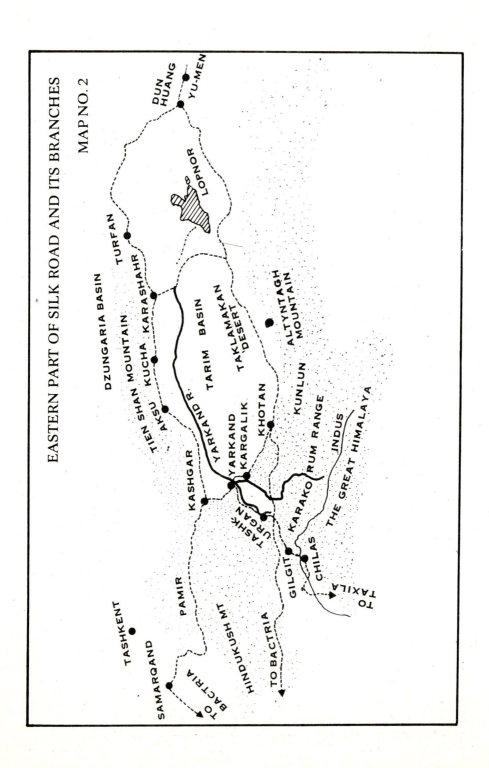

skirted the Gobi desert westward to Dun-huang, where it bifurcated into two — one passing the northern edge of the Tarim basin through the world-famous Turfan treasures, Aksu and on to Kashgar; and the second followed the southern edge at the foot of Kun lun and reached Khotan, Yarkand and on to Kashgar. The journey westward was either over the north of Pamir towards Samarkand or across the smaller valleys south of it through Wakhan, Badakhshan and onward to Bactria north of the Hindukush in the valley of the Oxus. It is the centres on the southern route that threw down paths across the Kun lun towards Karakorum region, opening a passage for trade to the Indo-Gangetic plains. From time to time the passage has varied, depending upon its starting point in Khotan, Qargalik or Yarkand, the eastern-most being the Khotan route across the upper valley of Yarkand river over to Kun lun. On the south it crossed the Muztag river and after passing through Shimshal reached the main channel of Hunza river. But a route from Yarkand proper would follow its tributary of Tashkurgan river and reach the town of that name and branch off either towards Wakhan or towards Khunjrab, the source of the Hunza river. It is the Wakhan route that can be reached directly from Gilgit, Chilas or Chitral over high passes.

Khunjrab is the starting point of the present Karakorum Highway, which gives, for the first time in history, an easy access to China's potential trade and intluence down to the Arabian sea and onward to the "free world". The older approach was across Klik Mintaka over to the opening of Misgar and onward to Hunza. Mintaka pass has been an opening towards the old Chinese cmpire on the east and Tsarist Russia on the north-west. The British in the subcontinent kept south ot it. Hunza became a pivot "where the three empires met." Hunza became proverbial for promoting longevity of human life but that is just for thc glacial climate away from the diseases of Ihe plains and the plenty. Hunza is the name and Rakaposhi is the glacier over which the fairies cast a charming look for those who care to unload the burden of human fatigue.

Chinese Pilgrim Route (Map No. 3)

Three famous Chinese pilgrims are known to have visited Karakorum region. Fa-Hian came here about A.D. 400. Sung-yun travelled between A.D. 518 and 520 and Hiuen Tsang visited between A.D. 630 and 640. Fa-Hian, whose original name was Kung, was a native of Wuyang ot the district of Ping-yang in the province of Shen-si. He started from Ch'angan in Shen-si, crossing the Lung mountains, reached the fortified town of Chang-yeh in Kan-suh, and finally reached Dun-huang, located at 39°30' N. Latitude and 95° East Longitude.

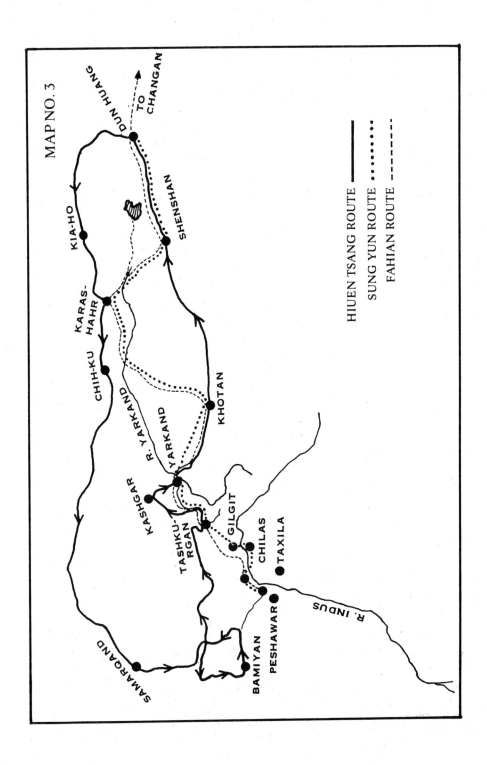

Thence he took the southern route south of the desert and came to Shen-shen or Cherchen of Marco Polo. From here he went northward along the Tarim river and came to Kara Shahr, which lies on the northern route and is identified with O-ki-ni of Hiuen Tsang. From Kara Shahr he again went south-west and reached Khotan. He then pressed on to Tseu-ho country, generally identified with Yarkand. From here he went south for four days and entered Tsungling (Kun lun) mountain. For twenty-five days he journeyed to arrive at Kie-Sha, to be identified probably with Tashkurgan, meaning Stone Tower. Having crossed Tsungling he entered the borders of the subcontinent, where there is a little country of Toli, or Talilo of Hiuen Tsang, usually identified with Darel valley but should be taken for the whole of Chilas zone. Journeying south-west for fifteen days he reached Udyan (modern Swat). The journey is thus described:

"The road was difficult and broken, with steep crags and precipices in the way. The mountain side is simply a stone wall standing up 10,000 feet. Looking down, the sight is confused, and on going forward there is no sure foothold. Below is a river called Sint-uho (Indus). In old days men bored through the rocks to make a way, and spread out side-ladders, of which there are seven hundred (steps) in all to pass. Having passed the ladders, we proceeded by a hanging rope-bridge and crossed the river. The two sides of the river are something less than 80 paces apart."

Sung-yun was a native of Dun-huang. He was sent on an embassy to the western countries by the Empress Dowager (Tai-Han) of the Great Wei dynasty to obtain Buddhist books. He traversed the whole of the Karakorum Region. First he arrived at the Chihling (Barren Ridge), the western frontier of the Wei kingdom. Proceeding westward twenty-three days and having crossed the Drifting Sands, he reached the country of Tuh-kiueh-hun (the Eastern Turks). From here onward he followed the southern route. Going west 3500 li he came to the city of Shen-shen. Still to the west 1040 li, he reached Tso-moh, probably in the vicinity of Cher-chen Then he went to Moh and ManMoh. The latter is identified with Pin-Mo. Next he arrived at Khotan. From here he proceeded to Chakuka, identified with Yarkand. Still to the west he reached the country of Han-Pan-to (i.e. Kabhanda), identified with Tashkurgan. Going west he ascended Tsungling mountains and then to the city of Kiueh-yu or Kong-yu. Further ahead he came to Puh-hoi mountains and reached the top of Tsung-ling, which was the last point of the kingdom of Han-Pan-to. Next he entered the kingdom of Poh-ho, which is described below:

"The mountains here are as lofty and the gorges deep as ever. The king of the country has built a town, where he resides, for the sake of being in the

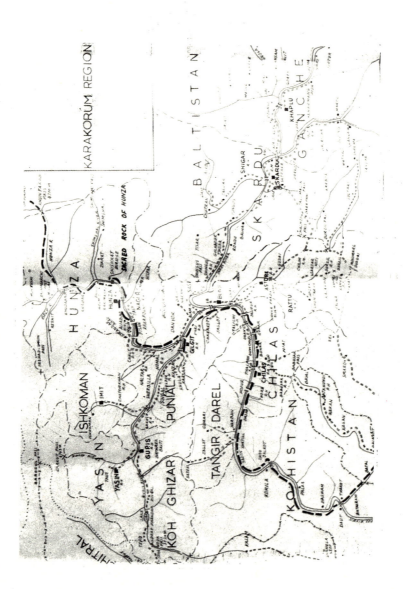

Map No. 4

Pattan : Two hunters

Pattan : Tiger pouncing upon a man

mountains. The people of the country dress handsomely, only they use some leathern garments. The land is extremely cold—so much so, that the people occupy the caves of the mountains as dwelling places, and the driving wind and snow often compel both men and beasts to herd together. To the south of this country are the Snowy Mountains, which, in the morning and evening vapours, rise up like gem-spires."

From the description this appears to be Misgar area, where caves are still seen and used for living purposes. If this identification is correct, Sung-yun must have crossed over the Mintaka pass.

Beyond this country lay the country of the Ye-Tha (Ephthalites), who "receive tributes from all surrounding nations; on the south as far as Tiehlo; on the north, the entire country of Lae-leh, eastward to Khotan, and west to Persia—more than forty countries in all." Next he entered the confines of the country of Po-sse, which should be identified with the northeastern part of present Hunza, where Wakhi is spoken. The next is the country of Shie-Mi. As he says: "This country is just beyond the Tsung-ling mountains. The aspect of the land is still rugged; the people are very poor; the rugged narrow road is dangerous - a traveller and his horse can hardly pass along it one at a time." The description suggests that it should be located round about modem Hunza valley. Further ahead mention is made of the country of Po-lulai, i.e. Bolor, usually taken for Gilgit area. From here he went to U-Changna, i.e. Udyan (modern Swat). In this journey, "they use iron chains for bridges. These are suspended in the air for the purpose of crossing (over the mountain chasms). On looking downwards no bottom can be perceived; there is nothing on the side to grasp at in case of a slip, but in a moment the body is hurled down 10,000 fathoms. On this account travellers will not cross over in case of high winds."

Hiuen Tsang was born in A.D. 603 at Ch'in Liu in the province of Honan. In search of good instructor he came to Changan, where, stirred up by the recollection of Fa-Hian and Chi-yen, he resolved to go to the western regions. From Ch'angan he went to Tsing-chau. From there he proceeded to Lan-chau, the provincial city of Kan-suh. He was then escorted to Liang-chu. This city was the entrepot for merchants from Tibet and the countries east of Tsungling mountains. Then he came to Kwa-chau, a town about ten miles to the south of Hulu or Bulangir river. Then he followed the northern route, which stretched towards the country of I-gu (Kamul) and finally came to Turfan. From here he went to O-ki-ni. i.e. Kara Shahr and then to Kuche. Passing through Baluka or Bai in the Aksu district he proceeded in a northerly direction across Icy Mountains into the plains bordering on the Tsing lake (i.e. Issyk-kul), then along the fertile valley of

Farm Animals

Su-yeh river to the town of Taras and thence to Nujkend and Tashkent (Sheshi). From here he proceeded to Sa-mo-kien or Samarkand. Next he went to Kashamia, half way between Samarkand and Bokhara and then to Pu-ho (or Bokhara). Finally, he reached Tami (or Tirmiz on the Oxus). After crossing the river he passed through several places on way to Bamiyan and Kapisi (i.e. Bagram near Charikar). Thence he came to Ningrahara, Gandhara and Udyan (modern Swat). It is from here that he passed on to Karakorum region, He describes:

"Going north-west from the town of Mung-kia-li (i.e. Mingora), crossing a mountain and passing through a valley, we reascend the Sin-tu river. The roads are craggy and steep; the mountains and the valleys are dark and gloomy. Sometimes we have to cross by ropes, sometimes by iron chains stretched (across the gorges). There are foot-bridges (or covered ways) suspended in the air, and flying bridges across the chasms, with wooden steps let into the ground for climbing the steep embankments. Going thus 1000 li or so, we reach the river valley of Talilo, where stood once the capital of U-chang-na. This country produces much gold and scented turmeric. By the side of a great sangharama in this valley of Ta-li-lo is a figure of Maitreya Bodhisattva, carved out of wood. It is golden coloured, and very dazzling in appearance, and possesses a secret spiritual power (of miracle). It is about 100 feet high, and is the work of the Arhat Madhyantika. This saint by his spiritual power caused a sculptor to ascend into the Tushit (Tu-si-to) heaven, that he might see for himself the marks and signs (on the person of Maitreya); this he did three times, till his task was finished. From the time of the execution of this image the streams of the law (religious teaching) began to flow eastward.

"Going east from this, after climbing precipices and crossing valleys, we go up the course of the Sin-tu river; and then, by the help of flying bridges and footways made of wood across the chasms and precipices, after going 500 li or so, we arrive at the country of Polulo (Bolor).

"The country of Polu-lo is about 4000 li in circuit; it stands in the midst of the great Snowy Mountains. It is long from east to west, and narrow from north to south. It produces wheat and pulse, gold and silver. Thanks to the

Kandia : Stylized ibex (bronze)

quantity bf gold, the country is rich in supplies. The climate is continually cold. The people are rough and rude in character; there is little humanity or justice with them; and as for politeness, such a thing has not been heard of. They are coarse and despicable in appearance, and wear clothes made of wool. Their letters are nearly like those of India, their language somewhat different. There are about a hundred sangharamas in the country, with something like a thousand priests, who show no great zeal for learning, and are careless in their moral conduct. Leaving this country and returning to U-to-kia-han-chan (Udakhanda), we cross at the south the river Sin-tu. The river is about 3 or 4 li in width, and flows south-west. Its waters are pure and clear as mirror as they roll along with impetuous flow. Poisonous Nagas and hurtful beasts occupy the caverns and clefts along its sides. If a man tries to cross the river carrying with him valuable goods or gems or rare kinds of flowers or fruits, or especially relics of Buddha, the boat is frequently engulfed by the waves. After crossing the river we arrive at the kingdom of Ta-cha-shi-lo (Takshasila)."

Hiuen Tsang's return journey was across the Pamir via Kashgar, Yarkand and onward along the southern route.

Pattan : Gold waistband

Journey Through Karakorum Highway

All historic routes from Central and Northern Asia to the Indo-Gangetic plain have converged on the old city of Taxila, correctly Taksha-sila (literally "the hill of the serpent (king Taksha")—a name which survives in that of the neighbouring hill Margala, correctly recorded by Alberuni as Mar-i-Qila, meaning "the (hill) fort of serpent". Margala bears Taxila on its western slope while on its eastern slope the modern capital of Islamabad spreads down to the river Soan, literally "the golden (river)". In the past Taxila was the main city, where came Alexander the Great, Sultan Mahmud of Ghazni and many others, while Islamabad, represented by several old ruins, was just a suburb. Today Islamabad is the main city while Taxila is growing as an industrial suburb. Nicholson Tower, built in honour of General Nicholson who fought in four wars but was killed in 1857, beacons the travellers to Margala pass through a saddle of the hill. Nearby is the old paved road, repaired in the time of Aurangzeb in 1672 by the orders of Mahabat Khan.

From Taxila three roads lead to Karakorum Highway. The first starts from Taxila Museum, passes through the old ruins of Sirkap, Jandiala, Sirsukh and the Buddhist monasteries of Mora Moradu and Jaulian and reaches Haripur via Khanpur, where a new dam is being built on the Haro river. The second goes through the main city of Taxila and passing through Heavy Mechanical Complex reaches the Highway five miles before Haripur. The third follows the Grand Trunk Road through Saraikala, where a Mughal caravan serai still stands on its right and on its left is the mound of the pre-Indus culture situated on the bank of the Kala rivulet. Onward the road kisses the beauteous spot of the Mughal Wah garden, leaves behind the Sikh shrine of Panja Saheb and then turns northward at Hasan Abdal, named after the Muslim saint Baba Hasan Abdal or Wali Kandhari, whose *ziarat* crowns the top of the hill. In the city we have an old Mughal garden, wrongly attributed to Lala Rukh, the so-called daughter of Aurangzeb. The road leads on to Haripur, and after joining with the other two proceeds to Havelian, named after the *Haveli,* residential palace, of a local chief, and onward to the picturesque hill resort of Abbottabad, a new city built a little away from the old Buddhist monastic settlement at Damkot, correctly Dharma-kot, not far from an old water spring on a by road leading towards the hills of Nathiagali and Murree. Further ahead is the main focal point of Mansehra, correctly Man-Shahr, the city of Man.

Mansehra Rock Edicts.

Rock Edicts of Mansehra

Mansehra lies at the junction of four roads. Besides the Karakorum Highway coming from Taxila and proceeding to the upper Indus valley, one road goes east to Kashmir and another to Kaghan, Nilam valley and onward to Babusar pass leading to Gilgit. It is therefore no wonder that the place was chosen for inscribing the fourteen rock edicts by the Mauryan emperor Asoka in the middle of the third century B.C. - the edicts which incorporate commandments of administration as well as of moral teachings. The granitic boulders, on which they are engraved, lie amidst the scatter of hill rocks to the north of the city. These rocks have now been cut through by the Karakorum Highway. One inscribed boulder lies to the left of the road and others to the right side, all under modern canopies, erected for the purpose of protecting the writing. But alas! the weathering has been so intense that reading is today almost impossible. The inscriptions are written in Kharoshthi script in the Gandharan Prakrit language. Asoka is not named here by name but only by his titles of *Devana Praya Priyadasi Raja* ("The king, beloved of gods, of noble appearance"). As an example of administrative measure, the following is taken from Rock Edict VI:

"Thus says King Priyadarsi, the Beloved of the gods:—A long time has elapsed, during the whole of that time no (proper) transaction of business or (proper) report was made before. So, I have so done that at all times whether I am eating, or, in the inner chamber, or in the cattle-shed (the station of herdsmen), or on horse-back, or in the garden—everywhere the reporters (or informers) should report to me the people's business. If I ever verbally command a man who causes any payment to be made, or who causes any injuction to be announced; or again, when I pass or place an order to the High state functionaries or Ministers on any matter of urgency and in that matter a dispute (or controversy) arises or a deliberation proceeds on in the Council—then irnmediately that affair should be reported to me in all places and at all times. Thus have I commanded. For, I never feel (full) satisfaction in my exertion and dispatch of business. For, the welfare of all people is regarded by me as the (chief) duty to do. And of that again the root is exertion and the dispatch of business. Because there is no other work more (essential) than the (act for the) welfare of the people."

On the appointment of special officers Rock Edict V says:

"Such *Dharma-mahamatras* were employed by me when I was consecrated thirteen years. They have been employed for the establishment of the law of piety among all (religious) sects and for the good and happiness of the *Dharmayutas* (the officers of the lower rank) through the growth and progress of *Dharma*. They are employed (specially) for the welfare and happiness of the Yavanas (Greeks), the Kambojas and the Gandharas, and also of those other people who are inhabitants of the western border, and of the hired servants and masters, of the Brahmanas and the wealthy people, and of the helpless and the old people, and they are employed also to free the *Dharmayutas* from hardship. They are employed to see to the counter-acting of the judicial sentence, freedom from hardship and the release of persons imprisoned, on the score of their being found to be attached to their children, or their being thrown overboard (hurled into misery) or their being older in age. Here (in the capital city) and other outside towns they have been everywhere employed in all the harems of my brothers and sisters and also over those others who are our kinsmen. Then everywhere in my dominion these *Dharma-mahamatras* are employed to see that the *Dharmayutas* are devoted to the Law of piety and are given to charity."

Of particular interest are his views of toleration recorded in Rock Edict no. XII:

"King Priyadarsi, the Beloved of gods, shows reverence to people of all religious sects, whether (wandering) ascetics or householders with gifts and various kinds of reverence. But (the king), the Beloved of the gods does not consider so much for gifts of reverence as that—what is it?—there should be a growth of the essence in all sects. But this growth of the essence has many aspects. But this is the root of that —namely, restraint of speech. What is that? That there should not be reverence (by over-rating) to one's own sect and disparagement (by under-rating) of other sects when no topic or occasion arises; or, they should be small (indeed) when this or that occasion arises. As all the other sects of reverence for this or that reason (or in different manners) By doing thus one promotes one's own sect and at the same time does good to other sects. By acting otherwise one injures one's own sect and does ill to other sects. That person who does reverence to his own sect and disparages other sects—does all this only out of attachment to his own sect—and why so? —with the intent that he should elevate his own sect. That (person) again by acting thus injures very greatly his own sect. So contact, however, is a good thing. How so? So that people belonging to different sects may hear and willingly hear the Law (of piety as adopted) by one another. For, thus, the desire of (the king), the Beloved of the gods, is—what is it?—that men belonging to all sects may become versed in many lores and stick to virtuous deeds. Whoever are faithful to particular systems (or creed) should tell others that (the king), the Beloved of the gods, does not so much care for gifts and (forms of reverence —how so?— as that there should be growth of the essence in all sects and that to a large extent also."

Hazara Plain to the Indus

Beyond Mansehra the hill outcrop vanishes and we tread along the Hazara plain - a country which is full of the memory of Abhisares, the opponent of Alexander the Great and the master mind responsible for planning many obstacles in the advance of the Greek invader. Abhisares not only saved his own country from Greek menace but also kept Alexander's forces busy west of the Indus river in the hill-girt region of Buner (see below). Onward the road passes through Sinkiari, a name which is sometimes associated with a people, called

Thakot: Indus view.

Shins, who are now living in the Gilgit area. But sober history does not substantiate this connection. As we proceed ahead the pine forest of Ichhrian greets our eyes and our road climbs higher and higher until we pass the first range of the Himalaya at Darra Farhad. Thereafter we enter the level plateau at some height, where the important place is called Chhatar Plain. Because of the height the local wells spring forth cold water for drinking. Further ahead there is again a climb along the winding road, which is lined with pine trees on its either side, until we reach the second range at Batagram, probably Baragrama (i.e. Big Village) or Baudha-grama (i.e. Buddhist village).

From Batagram petrol pump an approach road takes off towards Pemal Sharif on the right from the main Highway and leads onward to Pishora, about 6 km. away. Pishora actually lies on the Highway and can be approahced directly as we drive along. Here on the top of the village we meet with the ruins of the first settlement, much of which has now been levelled into fields. As we climb up on foot by a path we reach the top and witness many caves and pass by water springs, by the side of which the Buddhists built their *Viharas*. From the top a beautiful view of the whole valley can be had, with the village at the bottom and the Highway passing along a rivulet towards the pass of Kat Galai in front. The Pemal Sharif road comes from the top and reaches just close to it. Here we have a long tunnel, the access to which is difficult. However, there is a big overhanging cave, which has still preserved some hunting scenes as well as Buddhist paintings. They fall into two groups. The first group is drawn in white pigment with filled-in bodies which are drawn on the lefthand side. On the extreme left is a standing man in tight-fitting long coat and his hands at the waist. A bowman on foot is shooting an arrow. A horse-rider behind is also shooting from his bow. All the figures have turban on head in a style that speaks of mediaeval period.

The second group is painted in red. Two standing humans on right are standing in worshipful pose. To the left is a horse and above is a domical roofed building with two square hangings from the roof. A deer is seated at the door. Inside the house a man is seated on a high seat. To his right is a bird and to his left a dog. Another man is seated on a bench. Then we see a domical stupa with relic chamber and three umbrellas on its top and two lion pillars, one on either side. The Kharoshthi inscription on its either side reads: *Kanishka-maharaja suviharo*, i.e. the monastery of Maharaja Kanishka (the great Kushana emperor who ruled in the Ist-2nd century AD.). A second stupa of the same type with lion pillars is also seen nearby. There are several other house plans, humans and perhaps also the figure of a king.

As we descend down the Kat Galai pass, we suddenly come to an opening which brings into view the marvellous picture of the Indus river at Thakot (correctly Sthana-kot), on the right bank of which rises a steep hill towards Swat and Buner. This hill is crowned by the height of Pirsar, about five miles away from Thakot on the other side of the river. Sir Aurel Stein identifies this height with Aornos, the last stronghold west of the river Indus, which was besieged by Alexander the Great in order to haul the retreated soldiers of Swat with the connivance of Abhisares. According to Stein the mountain spurs descend steeply to the Indus opposite to the mouth of the Nandihar valley near Thakot. Pirsar is a serrated crest crossed by two passes. The summit of the Pirsar spur "presents itself for a distance of a little over a mile and a half as an almost level plateau, occupied along practically its whole length by fields of wheat. The width of the cultivated ground on the top varies from about 100 to 200 yards, with strips available for grazing by the side of the fields. Fine old trees form small groves in places, and one of these near the middle of the ridge shelters a much-frequented Ziarat, or shrine. There are several small springs in the little gullies that furrow the steep slopes close below the ridge, and these feed the streams that drain into the valleys below. Pirsar fort is now approachahle from Shangla pass by jep."

Right on the Indus there is a resthouse and a breathing space under the tree. Further ahead there is a bridge on the Indus built by the Chinese, which leads across the river into Kohistan and to the town of Basham, picturesquely situated on the Indus at the divide of two linguistic groups of languages, the Pashto on the right bank and Mahuar on the left bank. Basham resthouse is the pleasantest for the overnight stay. Basham is also the meeting place of two roads—one which comes from Swat over Shangla and the other the Karakorum Highway that comes from Thakot. Inside the Gorband valley towards Swat many remains of the late Bronze Age graves have been found.

Kohistan

Kohistan is the "Yagistan" (Unknown Track) of the British period. It was out of bound for the British as well as for many other governments that existed around in the past. It is the region which makes a real divide between the Himalaya, Hindukush and Karakorum. The river Indus, which in its upper reach flows east to west, now turns and bends down to the south. High mountains close up and throw fans of pleistocene deposits on their slopes, enticing man to build small fields ranged in terraces right upto the summit. The graded fields cover the slope and sometimes spread out in limited flats that make the high banks of the river. From sides several river torrents bring down melted water or spring water and push down shingles and rolled boulders in the form of landslides across the Karakorum Highway. These side valleys and terraced slopes of the mountains make up individual abodes of unknown tribes whose history goes back to hoary past. They are all kings unto themselves and form tribal and linguistic groups. Each one of them is recognisable by tall standing castles in the midst of the fields, which alone stand as a guarantee to their safe living. Basham is right on the heart of this zone and is a meeting place of cross roads and cross cultures. Pattan, literally "city", is now picturesquely located right on the bank of the Indus. Pattan is marked by the remains of an ancient fortress consisting of defensive walls, some residential quarters and watch towers, still visible from KKH at the bend of the Indus river. Here a chance discovery led to the find of a heavy weight girdle (weighing nearly 16 kg.) of gold. It is square in section, one face having a series of parallel lines, and three others have engraved human and animal figures. The animals include Stag, Horse, Ram, Ibex, Deer, Goat, Rabbit and Tiger. Among the birds, eagle is predominant. The humans are shown as hunters. The tigers are pouncing upon weaker animals or on men. No winged creature is depicted nor can we find any Indian influence on them. The animal styles appear to have link with the Scythian art of the Trans-Pamir region. The role of the humans alongwith the typical cap confirms this link. The girdle is now preserved in Peshawar Museum. At Komila or Dassu on either bank of the Indus we cross again the river and then follow on the left bank of the Indus into the most difficult passage of the past as the river breaks through several gorges but now made easy by blasting the hill and laying the road. At Komila we first meet the rock carvings just below the petrol pump right on the river side on several boulders but unfortunately the boulders have cracked and the carvings much destroyed. However they show some Buddhist carvings. On the other side of the Indus river a jeepable road takes one to a beautiful wooden mosque whose roof is now gone but beautiful carved pillars still exist. Closeby are old graves with carved wood coffins. In the past the travellers passed on to Sapat maidan by foot on their onward journey to Babusar, Chilas and Gilgit because the river side was very difficult to cross. Beyond Komila opens up Kandia valley, wherefrom Bronze Age material has been recovered. In the past this valley led to Swat across the high range of the Hindukush. Once Sir Aurel Stein also came here from Swat.

Shatial and Darel Valley

Furhter ahead the Indus river breaks through several gorges. The high mountains stand wall-like overhead. These gorges come to an end at Sazin, where we have a breathing space in a wider opening. About two miles away is the first interesting place at Shatial just where a new bridge spans the Indus river. The bridge gives access to two valleys—Tangir on the west and Darel on the east—both of which have rich archaeological material. However, just close to the Highway and not far from the bridge we meet with the first series of rock carvings that speak of the importance of the place in the past. This was the place visited by several travellers, missionaries and traders at least from the time when the first record in Kharoshthi script was engraved here in the first century AD. Several hundreds of inscriptions in the Sogdian language are found here. They give names of persons who came here from Samarkand, some on their way to China. One Chinese inscription on an isolated rock, very poorly drawn, has also been noted here. Inscriptions in Brahmi start from fifth century AD. onward. One rock gives a series of kings belonging to the *Khasa* tribe, suggesting that at least from the fifth century AD. the *Khasas* lived in this vicinity. Much earlier in the mid-third century B.C. the Mauryan emperor Asoka had to contend with the *Khasas*. Whether there was any other activity of Asoka in this part is not known. The Chinese pilgrims must have passed through this part but their description

Shatial : Close view.

does not give any definite information about this site. The carvings are spread out in several boulders and, besides engravings of horsemen and other hunting scenes, the most important is the drawing of a highly complex set of stupas and other figures on a flat rock.

The rock shows a big stupa, in the middle, of Central Asian type, a votive stupa on the right, and the story of *Sibi Jataka* depicted on the left. The builder of the main stupa has inscribed the name at the left bottom in Kharoshthi of the fifth century A.D. The inscription reads:

Dhamabai Jikhodarkha dhie ro thubu bato dhaditi

i.e. "the religiously devout daughter of Jikhodarkha established this best of stupa"

Another Kharoshthi inscription below speaks of "the gift of Chakshu, beloved of Sasa". This gift may refer to the votive stupa or to the depiction of the *Jakata*. In between the stupa carving there are several other inscriptions in Brahmi and Sogdian scripts, giving the names of persons.

The main stupa, in the middle, is approached by three steps with a devotee in Central Asian dress on its either siae. The steps lead to a plinth, on which there

Shatial : Stupa, close view.

are four stepped designs. From the end designs two columns rise up to support a horizontal beam, holding the dome of the stupa in the middle and pillars on sides. The dome has a further niche within. Bells hang down from the beam as well as within the niche and the dome. Above the dome is a series of umbrellas, from the top-most of which hang down banners on either side in an arch-like shape. Little bells are also placed at the ends of the umbrellas and also other points. The whole stupa presents a novel variety. The side stupa on the right is approached by four steps, leading to a tall base, on which is a solid pecked structure, triangular in shape, with umbrellas on its top, from which hang down twisted banners on either side. Here the triangular structure replaces the dome and thus makes another variety of the stupa. The depiction on the left side shows the Buddha, with flamed shoulders, seated within a cave, holding a dove in his lap. Below is a seat resting on a pedestalled pot, on either side of which is a devotee in the same style as on the main stupa. To the right a person is holding a balance in hand to weigh the flesh, obviously taken out from Buddha's body to save the life of the dove, thus illustrating the story of the Sibi *Jataka*. The devotees below appear to be father and daughter. On the right is the man in his tight-fitting dress and cap, with his hands in saluting pose. On the left is the daughter in long loose robe bent forward with flower in the left hand and incense burner in the rigt. On the whole the presentation makes an unusual embellishment and the scribblings in between speak of the great respect paid to the stupa.

Inside Darel valley old forts and fortified sites are met at Gayal, Phugach, Rajakot, Sivoker Kot and at other places right upto Manikyal. The Navakot at Phugach is made of mud pisse and belongs to a much later period. At Manikyal Bronze Age grave site has also been located, wherefrom old jars have been dug out by the local villagers. They are similar in concept as the Gandhara graves of the North-West Frontier Province. Of the Muslim period there are also some wooden mosques and old graves having decorated coffins and head-posts of wood. The mosque at Manikyal Payin is the best preserved but the one at Phugach has received later reconditioning. Unfortunatley old buildings over the graves of the five *Shahids* (martyrs) have been recently pulled down. The graves are still there. On the other side of the river yellow soil outcrop is pointed out as the place where the Shahids were killed. On that spot iron arrowheads are still found. Phugach is an interesting old village, where one can see the old house plans and also the old village plan. Here residential area is separated from the cattle enclosure. The wooden houses occupy upper storey for human living, the ground floor being reserved for store. The wooden pillars and doors are all carved. They show intricate geometric patterns and also some flower designs. Although these houses are built in recent years yet they carry forward the old tradition.

From Shatial to Thor

After Shatial we cross the Harban *nala,* a small rivulet that builds the Harban valley to the south of the Highway. The valley has a good tillage and pasture land. Further ahead several boulders are seen on either side of the Highway. Some of them bear inscriptions in late Brahmi. These inscriptions give the names of the Buddhist monks, Brahmins and other missionaries who moved about for the propagation of their religions. Sometimes we also get the carving of a stupa or a temple. Still further in between the Highway and the Indus river loose rocky outcrop is seen by the riverside. In this rock artificial caves have been excavated. In front of one of the cave some loose broken sculptured stones are lying. It seems that the caves were actually used by the Buddhists but today shepherds herd their animals during inclement weather. Further ahead right on the Highway, to its left, is a small outcrop (30 km from Chilas), which has a flat vertical surface on the western side. On this surface three animals are engraved. Two of them ibexes in local style but the third shows all the peculiarities of a Scythian prancing horse but it has curved horns on the head, suggesting that the intention was to draw an ibex. However, it has been modelled on the Scythian

Roadiside : Three ibexes, one in scythian style.

style of a horse. Nearby is a small boulder lying flat on ground, having a Kharoshthi inscription of first century B.C., reading *Magulaputrasa,* i.e. "Of Magulaputra". Still ahead is the site of Minargah where several inscriptions and animal carvings can be seen.

The Highway then passes through an opening in between the low hills, the river having receded to our left. And then we reach the big site of Thor, just at the point where this rivulet meets the Indus river. A small village of the Soniwals is now located here. The Thor valley opens out on our right. There are actually two sites, one on the right bank of the Indus river and the second on the left bank just below the modem bridge that spans the Thor rivulet. In the centre of the left bank site is a low outcrop of rocks containing several inscriptions in late Brami. But several other boulders are scattered in the vicinity right upto the Soniwal village bearing stupa carvings and inscriptions in early Kharoshthi and also in Brahmi. To go to the other side of the Indus river one has to cross by wooden rafts that can be hired from the village. There is a wide open sandy plain on a higher terraced bank of the Indus river. This higher terrace was occupied later in history as here we get all the inscriptions in later Brahrni and the temples associated with Brahmanic religion. In one place we have a nicely drawn peacock with the name of Vishnu Sena written on its top. In another place a crude temple is engraved alongwith *svastika* and trident figures above an earlier markhor and inscription, reading *Om Devadharmoyam Nandiyasya,* i.e. "This is the religious gift of Nandiya." The third shows a beautiful temple in the style of a stupa alongwith a crude fugure of a man with upraised hands and the name in the late Brahmi *Sri Vasudeva*. The fourth is a royal inscription reading *Simhadeva Jayati,* i.e. "Simhadeva conquers". Below is the name of a Buddhist monk Priyamitra bhikshu: In another place a peacock is holding a serpent by his beak and nearby is a Brahmi inscription of the fifth century A.D. There is also an isolated trident with the name of the donor *Sri Deva Chota.* Further ahead a man is standing beside a markhor. On the top is a Brahmi inscription reading *Khande Para-Surama.* Another boulder shows several ibexes of an earlier period and later inscription of Buddhist faith in two lines. It seems that Thor was an important centre in the past and continued to attract persons from a very early period right down to the first millennium A.D. Here one can study prehistoric carvings, animal drawings, Buddhist figures, Hindu temples and find inscriptions of kings, missionaries, and private individuals.

Hodur

From Thor we drive straight to Hodur (ten miles west of Chilas) where one can cross the Indus river by a bridge and reach the other side where archaeological remains are found. From the Indus bridge one can have a good view of the Nanga Parvat (Dyamar) if the sky is clear. As we proceed towards Chilas, the view gets obstructed by lower hills like Thak and Bonar but these again have snow-capped tops, which present a splendid panorama from Chilas by road if the light is faourable. The name Hodur is probably derived from that of a *durga* (fort) that stands on a ridge on the left bank of the rivulet that bears the same name. From the Highway the green fields of the village present an attractive scene on the other side of the Indus river. It is at the foot of the fort and all along the lower height of the hill towards the east, on rocks and boulders, that hundreds of carvings can be seen. The fort occupies a ridge that is cut away from the main hill on the north. The fortification wall follows the contour of the ridge and the approach is from the riverside . The old steps leading to the fort are now broken down. On the top is a citadel with round towers and on a lower slope are several living rooms, many of which contain broken querns and pestles. On the citadel some ashes and charcoal are also scattered, suggesting that at some time the fort was burnt; The location and the type of the fort appear to be similar and contemporary with the hillforts of the Hindu Shahis in North-West Frontier Province. It may be safely placed in the tenth century A.D. at the latest. However, no inscriptions and carvings have so far been found within the fort.

Two different types of carvings are seen in the lower range of the hills and on the outcrop that face the river Indus immediately. The first group is on the front outcrop. The carvings here continue the prehistoric tradition and show the hunting scenes of ibexes and markhors and humans, either singly or in groups, either hunting the animals or busy in some other work. All the fgures in this group are very crudely drawn. It is difficult to date them but some of them may go back to 1st and 2nd millennium B.C.

The second group belongs to Brahmanic faith and show several types of temples, derived from stupa model but distinguished from them by the fact that they end in *sikhara* (spire) and are crowned by a *trisula* (trident). Many of them are accompanied with inscriptions in late Brahmi of eighth century A.D. and speak of a Brahmin family which was responsible for the propagation of the Brahmanic faith. They are also accompanied by mounted horsemen and solar symbols. At several places a tiger with front right paw raised is drawn in a style that speaks of Sassanian art of Iran. In one place a sacred tree is drawn in dotted lines, towards which several horsemen are moving obviously in reverence. In other places humans are shown worshipping the temples. Subsidiary temples are also drawn in imitation of votive stupas. Such temples are also copied in thousands in crude drawings, suggesting the conversion of the masses of people. One remarkable representation shows probably a poor imitation of a Saivite deity with trident symbols characterising the fingers of the hands. The mounted horsemen are armed with cross bow and fan-shaped battle-axes, and they show great respect to solar symbols. It seems that both deities, Sungod and Siva, were objects of worship by these people. We also find here masked men in mysterious poses. On the other hand there is hardly any carving here that can be attributed to the Buddhists. It seems that Hodur was a stronghold of the Brahmin followers and that they had behind them large number of the local people that joined them alongwith their local tradition. The number of carvings at Hodur is so great and they are so wide-spread that the whole can be studied only by a prolonged study at the site.

From Hodur to Chilas

As we leave Hodur and proceed along Karakorum Highway (KKH) towards Chilas on the left bank of the river Indus, we have to slow down our speed as at every mile by the roadside inscriptions and carvings are seen on rocks and boulders. Simlarly on the other side of the river, after we cross over the hill to pass the intruded bend of the Indus river, we reach the open gateway, called Darbati, that leads on the right bank of the river Indus to the plain of Thalpan opposite Chilas town near the Thalpan bridge. On way there are several archaeological sites, some of which have been described further ahead.

To start with KKH, at the tenth Km from Chilas rnunicipal barrier, we notice the lower hill range quite close to the road on our right. On a flat rock surface, beside a modem writing, a Kharoshthi inscription gives the name of *Uvimadasakasa* — a name obviously referring to the second Kushana emperor Vima Kadphises. Although no royal title is attached to the name, yet identification should not be doubted as the writing belongs to that period and that this king is known to have conquered upto Ladakh. Above this writing an ibex is poorly drawn.

Further ahead, at the ninth km. from Chilas byroad, the opening is widened and the road passes through a wide plain fit for a camp site. On our left, i.e. the riverside, there is a low outcrop having no carvings but on our right the hills rise high and as we reach the 9th km, the inscriptions of later period abound on this

Chilas : Sword dance

side. The road has broken through some of the inscriptions but enough remains on the big rocks and boulders near the roadside. They fall in two groups one immediately on the roadside but facing the other way and hence not visible from the road but the second high on the rock surface facing the road. They give the names of the individuals, like *Kapila, Yasa, Sulota, Bhimaka* etc., or Buddhist names like *Bhikshu, Sramana, Sakya-bhrita* On this side there is also one Hebrew inscription on the top giving the name of a Hebrew merchant in a writing of the seventh centuly AD. The other group on the roadside gives the names of some kings, like *Jivavarnma, Jaja Chandraspala, Dharmaspala, Sura, Jinaspala, Sri Kumarasena, Tharangasena, Gajraja* etc. This second group of inscriptions begin in the fifth century AD. Among the second group the name Jivavarma Jaja recalls the same name of a Khasa ruler appearing at Shatial. All these inscriptions are in the late Brahmi character.

We leave behind these writings and proceed to the eighth km. from Chilas by road. Here the carvings are now seen on the left side of the road towards the river on the low hill outcrop and scattered boulders. Besides hunting scenes of markhor, stupa representation, we fnd several kinds of flowers carved on the top surface of a flat rock. Still more important are several inscriptions in Brahmi, some of which reveal the names of kings. One of them is Viravarma Jaja, obviously belonging to the Khasa tribe mentioned at Shatial.

We proceed ahead and come to the mouth of Gichi rivulet, which is seven km. from Chilas by-road. As we cross the bridge over this srnall rivulet, an outcrop of hill is seen on the Indus riverside. This is the most important spot from the point of view of archaeological remains.On the right side of the road there is a levelled ground, which appears to have been a Buddhist occupational site of the early centuries of the Christian era. But all this is now disturbed by road cutting. The earliest archaic carving is seen on the top of the hill on our left. It shows two humans hunting ibexes. As we come down from the top, we note a cleavage in the hill, which is now occupied by blown sands. Here one can also see quartz veins in the rock and broken nodules of quartz all over the place. In the sand one can also pick up worked quartz flakes, testifying that the place was a working platforrn of the prehistoric people. As we move towards the Gichi rivulet, we see a cave on this side, below which slopes down earth mixed with occupational soil. It is in this slope that rim fragments of broken pots have been recovered. These rim fragments belong to the same type of grave urns found in Darel valley. They may be dated to 1st millennium B.C. But of still more important are several stupa engravings, many of which are accompanied with inscriptions in late Brahmi of seventh century A.D. These carvings either face the

Chilas : Horsemen at ball play (polo)

road or on a slightly higher surface. The supas are very well drawn with flying banners. In some places long inscriptions are also seen. One inscription of *Amarasimha* gives grandiloquent royal titles to him. These carvings continue to the eastern extremity of the hill and then are further seen down below on the scattered boulders on the riverside. Some of the inscriptlons are very faint but a detailed study will reveal the names of several Buddhist missionaries who must have passed this way.

Beyond this site the road turns towards the river and right at the bend as well as down on the river there are several boulders by the side of three Muslim graves. These boulders again contain archaic hunting scenes as well as Buddhist inscriptions of later period. We can walk along the sandy plain and discover some more carved boulders or we can climb back to the road and drive another kilometer and come to the next important site, generally known as *Deva* site from the fact that one huge boulder, to the left of KKH, has a giant figure of a hurnan drawn in archaic style.

The site is nearly five km. from Chilas by-road. In order to see the carvings we have to go down to steep slope from the road. At flrst we get two carved boulders amidst several others which are plain. One big boulder is carved on all the sides and also on the top surface with archaic figures and inscriptions of later periods.The earliest are the prehistoric engravings of animals, hunting scenes—most of the animals are shown in a bi-triangular style. These figures are rather dim. Above and over them are later inscriptions, giving the names of individuals. The latest inscriptions belong to mediaeval period and are written in proto ..agari character. They appear to be the names of persons who were perhaps brought here for burning. If this is correct, the site must have been used for burning ghat for some time. The other big boulder has, on its top surface, giant figure of a human, besides palm and foot impression. The giant figure is of an unusual type, whose face is not properly drawn but bristling hair on head is quite clear. The hands are outstretched. He is putting on a skin loin cloth, to which a tail has been attached. The legs are straight down with feet turned outward but tied. At some later period breasts were added to this demoniac figure. It is difficult to date it but certainly it is in the archaic style and appears to be a concept of prehistoric period. When we leave these two boulders and approach riverside, there are several other boulders which show stupas and other scenes. Some of the boulders are arranged in some order, suggesting that they were held with veneration by the local people at some time in the past.

We can come back to the Highway and drive one kilometer and come to two or three sites on either side of a dry *nala*. Before the *nala* there is a great pile of boulders on either side of the road. The boulders towards the left side of the road have engravings of different periods. As we get down the road on the plain, the engraved boulders are seen for about fifty yards. One boulder gives a Kharoshthi inscription recording the name of *Veghaha Saka.* Other boulders give late Brahmi inscriptions and crude human drawings. At one place there is the name of *Priyamitra Bhikshu..* On another boulder the same *bhikshu* (monk) writes a long inscription in praise of the Buddha and gives the name of (probably a local ruler) *Chandrasura.* We also get the figures of warriors armed with cross-bow. We also get the names -of *Simhavarmanasya putra* (son) and of *Sri Jivadharma.* Another shows the figure of a goat with an inscription, *Sri Vahadevasya,* i.e. "Of the deity Sri Vahadeva", suggesting that this was the name of the deity represented by goat. Of still more important are the prehistoric carvings. Several boulders show palm and foot impressions. But one boulder is remarkable. This has carvings of two periods. Of the later period is a Buddhist stupa being worshipped by a standing person in an unusual dress, very beautifully drawn, Beneath these are the earlier prehistoric drawings very dimly visible. There are actually five humans represented, each one in a different style. The extreme left one shows the body formed by two long triangles joined at their apex with bristling hair on top and lower ends of the triangles making legs. Four points are seen at the meeting of the apex. The second human is also made up of two triangles, one on the top of the other, with the head and hands just marked. The third has a better portrayal of man in solid body and legs. The fourth is very crudely drawn but the fifth has again solid filled body. These prehistoric carvings carry forward the tradition seen at the earlier *Deva* site.

When we cross the dry *nala,* we come to the next site Two inscribed boulders are just below the electric pole. One gives the names *of Buddharakshita* and *Kumarasena* in late Brahmi but the other records, in Kharoshthi, the monastery of (Buddha's) foot-print (erected by) the monk Vaghea Ashagrea. On this stone Buddha's foot-print is also drawn. But for more carvings we have to go down to the riverside.

At the mouth of this very dry *nala* huge boulders are thrown asunder. On the flat surface of the rocks some important prehistoric carvings are seen. They are very dimly visible. One shows a couple in copulation in a peculiar style. The other shows standing humans, one big and another small in size with breasts, probably man and woman. By their side is a net pattem. At other places are palm and foot impressions. In one place a ladder is also shown. It seems that these pre-

Chilas : Bodhisattvas beside a stupa.

Chilas II: Two more individually

historic carvings represent a family settlement at this site. As we walk along the sandy plain towards the east, we come across several boulders with carvings of stupas, mounted horsemen, circles, ibexes, markhors, temples in actual worship by standing devotees, fan-shaped battle-axes and several inscriptions. One flat rock has a prominent figure of an ibex drawn in a ritual style suggesting that the ibex was an object of worship for the people at this late historical period when inscriptions were written here. The whole site on the low terrace of the Indus river is a suitable place for human habitation. it is along the dry *nala* that the prehistoric men must have hunted animals.

We come back to the Highway and just half a mile before Chilas by-road we get down and proceed towards the Iridus river. Here carvings are seen in different terraces. Somewhere Buddhist stupas and inscriptions are engraved but at other places some unusual representation of animals and birds are seen. At one place a goat is fighting with a snake. At another place there is a herd of lambs on one face of a rock and on the top surface some cattlepens and on the other face two pair of mother and father lambs are seen, one on the top of the other, perhaps with the intent of copulation. Nearby there is another boulder which shows a mother bird *(Chakor)* feeding a baby bird seated on a branch of a tree A little distant to the west there are two big boulders. One of them shows several types of circles with intemal divisions and dots, crude version of temples, fanshaped battleaxes and also humans. The other big boulder is still more interesting. Here we find, besides temples and stupas, two rows of men, each holding a sword in hand overhead. In between there are other men who are exercising with sword around their body. The whole scene represents a sword dance, for the first time seen in art in this part of the world. From here when we go down to the lowermost terrace just close to the river, we fmd a pile of rocks. One of them has a flat steep surface on the riverside. This surface is almost plain but for a peacock, a very faint stupa, and some animals. On the other hand the southern face of these rocks present a new picture of life that must have been present here from seventh century AD. onward. It seems that the riverside face at this time was drowned in the river flood and hence it was hardly used. The southern face shows the life of a people who ride on horseback by proving extreme dexterity in horse-riding and dancing on horse back, and use fan-shaped battle-axe as their symbol or flag. They were worshippers of the sun and also of the wheel of Vishnu and even trisula (trident) and phalus of Siva. In other words they were followers of the Hindu faith of a type that was popular in this region. They engraved temples on boulders. Here on this site there are several inscriptions in late Brahmi which give their names in the Sanskrit style. Starting from the eastern side we get several types of symbols, bottleshaped temples, battle-axes,

Chilas : Roadside stupa

Chilas : Worshipper beside a stupa.

circles, dented battle-axe enclosing an ibex within, men dancing around battle-axe, humans with cross-bow in hand, a unique horse-rider standing on a horse holding a balance in hand overhead, ending in trident symbol, a double circle with a star inside, two men fighting with battle-axe, another stupa on which stands a battle-axe, a late drawing of an elephant with a man seated on his head. Among several horseriders two scenes are very important. One shows double-headed python in a furious mood and the other shows a group of four horse-riders bent on playing a game of points. This may be the earliest representation of polo in art. On the westernmost part there are elaborate stupas with birds. The whole depiction presents the daily life of the people who probably introduced polo game, sword dance and dancing on horseback.

Chilas

From the last site we can directly pass to the next site about three hundred yards to the east on the lowest terrace close to the Indus river. In fact during summer when water level rises because of the melting of snow, the river comes to the very foot of the hill. It is here on the sandy banks that Soniwals wash gold from the sand.

Chilas : City general view.

The modern town of Chilas is removed two miles up to the south of KKH and is approached by a by-road, where at present there is a municipal barrier. Its nucleus is an old fort which was renovated, almost rebuilt, during Dogra Regime. The importance of the town increased as it gave access to Babusar pass wherefrom one can go to Kishenganga valley in Kashrnir or towards Hazara. The town is situated on the bank of the Butogah rivulet. In fact the oldest village was a fortified settlement known as Kot Butogah. It is near this old settlement that Soniwals made their own village called Soniwal Payin. This village occupies an older settlement, today recognised by several boulders bearing inscriptions and other carvings and particularly two large boulders having royal inscriptions and also the old name of the city *Somanagar*. This name of the town is repeated as Vira *Somonagara* at the Thalpan bridge on the right side of the Indus river in a writing of the fifth century AD.

Chilas is the most interesting place for study. Here one can spend days and go round several sites to learn about the wealth of the data of different periods. One can go along the Butogah rivulet and find carvings of circles, mounted horsemen, battle axes on many boulders on either bank of the rivulet. Similarly one can go along Thak *nala* and see the carvings but many of them are now gone.

Chilas : Giant demon-gon.

On the open plain of Thak das in between the two rivulets there is a high terrace where several boulders have stupas and inscriptions engraved on them. Even along the by-road that comes from KKH towards the town we meet with carvings on boulders on our right and left. These carvings show mounted horsemen, circles, and battle-axes. Even within the town, just close to the old rest-house there are some boulders bearing several varieties of designs. These stones have obviously slipped dowh from the top. Many of the stones have been broken and removed at the time of levelling for modern construction.

As we leave Chilas town and drive towards Soniwal Payin, we stop by a school and walk down to the edge of a terrace. Right there are two huge boulders. One of them has innumerable drawings of fan shaped battle-axes, ibexes, markhors and humans belonging to different periods. Local children have copied some of them on.other boulders in recent years. The second boulder again shows battle-axes, men holding cross-bow and battle-axes in hands and mounted horsemen. Some of them holding the same weapons in hands are actually standing on horseback. They remarkably well represent the spirit of these battle-axe people, who are now completely forgotten by the local people. However, we have traced them earlier at Hodur and at several other sites on way to Chilas.

When we walk eastward from this place about half a mile, we begin to get potsherds scattered in the fields until we reach a spot where we see two huge boulders standing aloft facing eastward. These two stones are lying in situ as they were originally placed They are historic memorials to the everlasting city of Chilas. Both of them bear inscriptions in Brahmi of sixth century AD. Some earlier inscriptions are also seen in the bigger stone on the left. The top line inscription on the left stone is a beautifully calligraphic piece written in royal hand. The inscription speaks of the conquest of the local ruler *Sri Vaishravana sena,* who bears the royal title of *Sakra-bhattaraka Maharajadhiraja.* The names of his two ministers are also given along with the name of his teacher *Rudra Sri,* who is said to have been established in the *Vishaya* (district) of *Silvata,* a name which comes closer to the place name *Siltas,* as given by Alberuni. It seems that at this time Silavata was the name of the area and the town was named *Somanagar.* The modern name Chilas appears to have come from Silavata. The second stone on the right gives the names of the rulers, apparently the forefathers of Vaisravana sena. We can proceed further ahead and see amid several boulders some more carved stones with drawings of stupas and other figures. The entire area is at a higher ground and below spreads the green fields right upto the petrol pump which is by the side of KKH.

Chilas : Roadside, Manjusri in between Stupas

Standing on the height of this old spot we can see the village of Butogah on our right, and as the rivulet bearing that name crosses KKH, there is a small outcrop of hills which contains several inscriptions, including the famous inscription of the Parthian ruler Gondophares and hence this low hillock is named Gondophares Rock. Still to the right is the hill of Jayachand which is full of inscriptions and Buddhist panels. In between, on the left side of KKH, there are other boulders bearing stupas, Buddhist *Jataka* stories and other royal inscriptions until we reach Thalpan bridge, on both sides of which are several engravings. On the other side of the Indus river spreads Thalpan plain, which is a mine of engraved stones, spreading right upto the Khinnar rivulet and even beyond the Thalpan village on its southern side. Continuing our journey westward from Thalpan plain we can proceed along an old path, generally named as Pilgrim Path, and witness the wealth of carved stones, prehistoric, historic, Buddhist, Hindu and Battle-axe people - all leading towards Hodur. On way we cross the occupational site of now-deserted village of Thakot, two Ziarat sites and two Khomar sites deep within the hill enclaves. Where Thalpan bridge now stands, there was also an old village which was washed away in the flood of the last century. This place appears to have been an old crossing. From here one could go to Gilgit along Khinnar *nala* and over the pass. Coming back to KKH, one can view the municipal barrier near the by-road to Chilas, beyond which several terraces lead us to the Indus bank. On these terraces some carved

Chilas II: Chinese inscription.

boulders are also seen. Near the river there is an outcrop of rocks which bear, from the chronological point of view, the earliest historic carvings of Chilas. This was the place which we left earlier when we came from Hodur in our last stop. We begin from this site where we left and give some details oi the vast historic material.

Chilas II

This site has ,been named Chilas 11 as it was discovered later, the first site being Jayachand hill, named as Chilas 1. It is on the lowest terrace of the Indus and the carvings are: (i) on the river face; and (ii) on the southern face. The carvings in the first category fall earlier in sequence and are datable by the Kharoshthi inscriptions that accompany them The carvings in the latter category are later in date and are datable by the Brahmi inscriptions that are found on the southern face. However, over the first category of carvings there are, at some places, late carvings done on the top of the older drawings. In between are some crude hunting scenes and other animals that fill the space. The carvings of the first category are alrnost all Buddhist in nature and present to us the form of Buddhism that prevailed here in the first century B.C. Only two Hindu deities Baladeva and Vasudeva are represented here twice in full iconographic details.

Chilas II : Hunting scene

Chilas II : Earliest seated Buddha.

The carvings of the second category show hunters, armed with different kinds of weapons, fighting scenes, circles, temples and other structural specimens, like tall towers with flames burning on top. These flamed towers appear to copy Zoroastrian ziggurats, and if this identification is correct, they must be post-Sassanian in date. In view of Iranian style of tigers seen at Hodur, which form a part of this cultural milieu, the Sassanian influence is quite reasonable to infer in these cases.

The riverside carvings are an interesting study. On the extreme left is a seated human figure in outline, holding a bowl in hand and a second standing person to his left in the act of offering a bowl to the seated figure. The figure is described in the Kharoshthi inscription as Bodhisattva (Buddha-to-be). The whole scene may represent the Buddhist legend of offering of a bowl to the Bodhisattva.

Chilas II : Double stupa.

The next scene to the right is most remarkable as it shows, above an earlier hunting portrayal, the representation of a historic scene, in which the seated figure on a high seat, named as Moga Raja (i.e. the Scythian ruler Maues) is being presented by his soldiers in Scythian dress, the captured fat ruler on the right, named as Gopadasa, who is being brought in chains. Below are his two sons, named Balaputra and Akshaputra. Still to the left is a simple stupa. The representation for the first time affords direct proof of the conquest of this region by the Scythian ruler, who appears to have come here from a northerly route.

Moving on further to right we see two stupas, one of them has a pillar on its either side and the other is topped by a crescent and a circle probably representing sun. To the left of this stupa there is another sun motif. A Kharoshthi inscription gives the name of Raghubira as its donor. Still to the right is a long Kharoshthi inscription again referring to the Scythian monarch Moga (Maues) and his governor Ghoshamitra. We get two more names Kaka and Samudrasena, who were related to the governor. To the right of the inscription is a standing man holding a relic casket in hand and a stupa by his side. He may be one of 'the persons named in the inscription. But a later carving of fan-shaped battle-axe and a man standing on horse has spoiled part of the inscription. Below

Chilas II: A pilgrim on March

Chilas II : Vasudeva and Baladeve

Chilas II: Scythian soldiers before a stupa.

the inscription other animals and mounted horsemen of a later period are engraved.

Still to the right we get elephant and stupas in outline, Bodhisattva seated in meditation pose, and below them three standing figures beside fan-shaped battle-axe, mounted horsemen and other animals of later period. The extreme left figure, which is crudely drawn, is named as Bodhisattva. Out of the remaining two, the left one, who is holding a discus in his right hand is called Vasudeva, and the right figure who is holding a spear on a plough base, is called Baladeva. Above the Hindu deities we have a double stupa and still above a seated figure of Buddha, the first appearance in the region. On the extreme right end of this face is a memorable representation of a Buddhist monk approaching with an incense burner in hand to worship before a stupa. The monk is named Buddharakshita. On the top is another pilgrim walking to left with a load hanging behind his stick on the shoulders. In his right hand he is holding a water jar. The pilgrim appears to be a Central Asian man.

In front of this tall rock there is a flat boulder bearing several figures of horsemen, hunting scene and inscriptions. These carvings are continued further towards the river. At one place there are two important representations. One is

Chilas II: Horse-rider above Kharoshtti inscription..

that of a standing human with his head formed by a stupa. He is named in the Kharoshthi inscription as *Sakamuni* i.e. the Sage of the Sakya tribe (meaning Buddha). The second is again a worship of the stupa by a monk, who is named Onivastara of Pusia.

Turning again to the river side we find several inscriptions in Kharoshthi, again naming Mahataka Moga (i.e. the Great Maues) and his another governor Sidhalaka besides Kaka and Budharakshita. Further ahead is a stupa on a base having three umbrellas on its top belonging to Sivadasa. Then we get another stupa erected by Bahae and Vataida.

In the next recess we get a totemic figure on legs besides a standing column but named as Hariti, a Buddhist deity. Above is a three-line Kharoshthi inscription of the Kushana king Vajheshka. Further ahead we get another stupa to which Scythian soldiers are approaching in reverence.

Another recess shows a stupa with two shells and a flight of steps. Below this stupa is a standing human, named Siva. Another inscription on the top says, "The god *Isa, Mahesvara* of Vareamaha." There are more stupas on the right. But the most important is the one of Rahula who is said to be *Mejupriya*, i.e. Iover of

Chilas II : Seated Buddha.

Chilas II : Krishna and Balarama

Chilas II : King Maues and soldiers.

Chilas II : Saka-muni.

the Madhyamika school of Buddhism. To the left of this stupa is a beautiful pillar and below the stupa are a bull and three horse-riders beside an incense burner.

At the end we find again two standing humans with a flowing dress covering the body. The left figure has a crown on head and a plough-topped banner in hand. The right figure has a crescent-topped head-gear and is having a discus in his left hand. The Kharoshthi inscription on top gives their names as (Bala) rama and Krishna.

This whole repertoire at Chilas II presents the Buddhist religious devotion with which these carvings were made in the first century B.C. The figures of Baladeva and Vasudeva are very interesting. It is only the southern face that presents an entirely different picture of a period when mounted horsemen were already in the scene.

Chilas II: Worshipper before a stupa.

Gondophares Rock

When we leave Chilas 11 and climb up the stony path towards the municipal barrier, several big boulders are seen on way. Some of them are carved and inscribed. One boulder shows a jumping horse drawn in outline. Another big boulder shows hunters, fighting men, temples, circles, mounted horsemen and several other designs. As we leave the municipal barrier and proceed eastward along KKH, we get other boulders in the vicinity of Brigadier Aslam's house. Two of them on the right side show some writing. On a blackish stone we find eight temples carved on three faces and one human. Another stone also shows some writing. On the left side of KKH four stupas are carved and also an inscription *Gajarajesvara*. Other stones showing hunting scenes and animals are scattered in several places. After seeing these odd stones we pass on to Gondophares Rock. There are actually two parts of the rock, the eastern and the western and also some odd stones standing alone. The inscription of Gondophares is on the eastern part on an odd standing stone. A human is drawn on the right hand. On the top the Kharoshthi inscription reads:

Vitaspa priyati Guduvharasa raja
i.e. "Beloved of Vitaspa, King Gondophares"

One boulder has one horse-rider and two more designs. Another has two indistinctive signs. On a slope of a huge pile of rock just by the river Indus several drawings of temples, stupas, battle-axes are intermixed with humans and circles. On a little higher level can be seen mounted horsemen holding battle-axe. In another place twelve battle-axes and several circles are drawn. One fallen stone has two beautiful stupas upside down, circle and cross. On a still higher rock surface two late temples on a pedestal can be seen and nearby are inscriptions in proto-nagari character, giving names of individuals. The temples are interesting as they enclose a fetish object within. If we pass on to the western part of the rock, the carvings are scattered in several places. Some are at great height and can be approached by scoops in the rocks, which served as steps. It is here that we have later Brahmi inscriptions, stupas, horsemen and battleaxes. At the sloping surface of a rock that is close to the Indus river there are several stupas of different periods. One stupa or temple has a tapering base marked by several horizontal lines within and topped by a small jar and crowned by a trident with flying banners on its either side. A human arrned with cross bow is standing below on right. Another stupa has an inscription saluting Buddha and is the work of *Balavira*. Thus Gondophares Rock was in continuous use from 1st century A.D. to at least fifteenth century A.D.

Chilas I

As we cross the Butogah rivulet and proceed eastward along KKH, we see Jayachand hill on our right, on our immediate left is a series of outcrops of low range and further ahead the hill on the riverside, on which Thalpan bridge now hangs. Thus actually there are three sub-sites and all of them are included under Chilas I. At the edge of Jayachand hill one can see the old footpath which led to Chilas from Thalpan. The first sub-site, Chilas Ia, on the left of KKH, is marked by a tall stupa carved on a surface facing west. It is visible right from KKH. This is the arch-type of a beautiful stupa erected on several terraces and topped by a series of umbrellas with name of the donor as Kubera-vahana. This is the work of seventh century A.D. but later in about 9th century A.D. the big word *Sri* was engraved on the top of the erlier inscription. Around this very rock and on the isolated boulders to the north there are some more stupas carved on flat surface along with inscriptions. As we pass on to the next rock, we find a different picture. In one alcove, at some height, there is a beautiful stupa of the type described before and hence belonging to seventh century A.D. But below it there is a later inscription written in proto-nagari script of ninth-tenth century A.D. It gives the history of the Shahi rulers of this part, the first king being *Sri Vajra*

Chilas II: Galloping horse

Chilas : Buddhist panel with a worshipper

Sura who had two princes *Simgha Sura* and *Vyaghra-Sura,* the latter having the titles of *Mahapilupati* and *Mahagajapati* (both meaning "the great lord of elephants") and the great minister Gikisila. There are other slightly later inscriptions in the neighbourhood, which give the names of individuals and also of some kings of the *Sura* family. Among the names of the individuals there are some which still survive among the Shina people of the region. Some of the individuals may be those who were perhaps burnt here after their death. If this is true, the place may have been used as burning *ghat.* In any case there is a local tradition that urn burials were found in the vicinity in the past.

We move on to the next rock, and amid several carvings of stupas, inscriptions and a human head we get one very important panel as the scene depicted here is the only one of this kind in this part. This illustrates the rare *Jataka* story of the "body sacrifice" of the Bodhisattva Mahasattva, labelled in the inscription on the top right as *Vyaghrani dharma nyayam,* i.e. "the principle of duty to tigers". Here in the centre is a tall stupa of the type seen before, with a devotee kneeling down on the left. Another devotee is prostrating on the right bottom. Above this devotee the Bodhisattva is lying flat on ground and on his body is the hungry lioness along with her cubs, eating the flesh of the Bodhisattva, who had voluntarily offered his flesh to feed the hungry animals. Still above the Bodhisattva is shown twice in the middle, once talking to the tree deity on the left and second time talking to *dikpala,* the deity of the quarters. The representation is a moving picture of sacrifice, befitting the local region, on the part of Buddha-to-be to save the life of animals.

When we proceed further eastward, we note KKH cutting through Jayachand hill. Carvings are seen both on the part on the riverside (Chilas Ib) and on the other part on the hillside (Chilas Ic). Today a footpath has been cut through the riverside part and it leads to Thalpan bridge. Along this path one can see several stupas carved on small scattered stones or on rocks. Somewhere there is a horse and at another place a mounted horseman. There are a few faint inscriptions as well. This series of carvings continues right upto the point where the peg for holding the strings of the bridge has been pierced into the rock. Just below KKH there is a broken figure of the Buddha. Only two of its pieces were recovered. The third piece which had part of the head is unfortunately gone. This is the figure of the seated Buddha on a raised pedestal in dhyani pose, with folds of the garment in semi-circular folds over the seat. A double trefoil arch, in the Kashmiri style, with golden plates in between the arches, surrounds the whole body of the Buddha. It may be placed in the seventh century AD. A little further down there is a still more beautiful engraving on a rock facing north. It shows the seated figure of the Bodhisattva Manju Sri in the top middle with an inscription in the late Brahmi to right, speaking of the salutation to the deity; a beautiful contemporary stupa to left below which an inscription saying that it was made by the king Simhadeva, and another later stupa to the right with an inscription below saying that it was done by Jivadharma. Further ahead there is another stone, on which we find a seated figure of Bodhisattva Manju Sri in the pose of fearlessness. This is also in the Kashmiri style as the flamed trefoil halo encloses the entire body.

Right opposite, across KKH, on the hillside (Chilas Ic) there are numerous carvings. spread over right from the roadside to the top of the immediate rocks. As we come along KKH from the town, first we see a goat at a height and below it a faint Kharoshthi inscription in Kushana style, reading *Kshatrapasa* Enakasa, i.e. "of the governor Enaka". Still above there is a small animal, probably a jackal, chasing an ibex with curved horns. Proceeding further ahead, we see, again on a top surface, a seated figure of the Buddha, with simple trefoil arch, in the Kashmiri style, enclosing the whole body, although the garment covers both the shoulders as seen in Gandhara style. If we look upward on our right, we will see a large surface of the rock facing east. Here we have a long interesting panel. All the figures are carved in the Kashmiri style. Right in the middle is a stupa of

Chilas II: T'ang Horse

seventh century A.D. in the local style. On lts left is a seated figure of Manju Sri, with an inscription speaking about the salutation to this deity as well as to *Tathagata* (i e. Buddha), seen on the right side of the stupa, by the king Simhadeva, who is seated below with a rosary in his left hand and a lamp in the right. The noble demeanour of the king is realistically shown. The Buddha on the left side is seated but it appears to have been drawn as an after-thought as it impinges on the stupa structure. To the extreme right is the standing figure of the Bodhisattva Maitreya holding a water pot in hand. On the extreme left the seated figure of Lokesvara in *abhaya* (fearlessness) pose is engraved with its own inscription to the left speaking about the salutation of king Simhadeva along with his wife. Some later carvings are seen still to the left.

Moving further eastward we come to a tall rock. Its top northem surface has a beautiful terraced stupa with a person worshipping at the left. The inscription on the right gives the name of the person as Priyasura. As we move to the eastern face of this rock, we find two standing Bodhisattvas, a *purna-ghata* (lucky jar) and an inscription of the king Simhadeva. The left-standing figure is that of Lokesvara and the right one is that of Maitreya. Both of them are in Kashrniri style. The inscription below the left figure speaks of salutation to Avalokitesvara and that below the right figure reads *Bauddha samana surena,* i.e. "by the hero of the Buddhist monks".

As we climb up still higher, we get several carvings of stupas, conch-shell and also inscriptions on rocks. But a separate isolated boulder has a Chinese inscription on a surface looking east. The inscription includes only four signs.

Chilas II: Worshipper before a stupa.

Thalpan Plain

As we cross the Thalpan bridge, we find, immediately on our right, some inscriptions carved on the rock facing north. One of them in the Brahmi character of 5th century AD. gives the city name *vira Somonagara*. From here we can go eastward and come to two rock piles about a hundred yards away. The western rock is exclusively devoted to the carvings of mounted horsemen, circles, battle-axes and other signs associated with them. But the eastern and northern portions have earlier carvings of stupas and Buddhas, although some of them have later carvings as well. At one place there is just one head drawn and above it is the story of the First Sermon of Buddha at Sarnath represented. It is because of this story that the site is called "Rock of the First Sermon". Here Buddha is seated in the middle while his five disciples are around him and below is the wheel of law on a pillar with a deer on its either side. The figures are drawn in an entirely different art style but derived from Gandhara school of 5th century AD. At another place the same disciples are sitting under a tree beside a stupa, probably representing the occasion when after being dissatisfied with the sage Buddha, who had become dischanted with the method of penance, had deserted him before Buddha obtained his final enlightenment. A third scene shows a seated Buddha with fat Vajrapani standing beside him holding a thunderbolt in

Thalpan : Central Asian prince before a stupa.

hand over his head. A fourth scene presented the seated Buddha in the *varada* (boongiving) pose with later stupas on right and left. Another important scene shows a faint representation of *Mara* scene, in which Buddha is seated in the middle and the two daughters of Mara (the god of temptation) are dancing, one on each side of the Buddha, with Mara himself looking furiously at the Buddha. At another place there is also a carving of Nestorian Christian Cross.

From here we can wander over the sandy plain and pass from one boulder to another admiring the carvings of the stupas, temples, and inscriptions on them. These boulders have been lying there for centuries. One such boulder, right in the midst of the plain, has a Chinese inscription along with stupa carvings. There are also concentration of engravings on different rocks. Such concentrations can be seen on either side of the Khinnar rivulet to the east right upto Thalpan village. A detailed examination will give names of several individuals, ministers, kings and monks. Just at the foot of the hill on the eastern part of the sandy plain there are

Thalpan : Deva approaching Buddha.

remains of stone masonry walls belonging to an earlier Thalpan village, which has been long given up. Here some old Muslim graves can also be seen. Another concentration of boulders is seen on the western side close to the hill. This pile has been called "Altar Rock" because of the fact that the group of rocks make some sort of a shrine. It is here that we have a Kharoshthi inscription of the Kushana period reading *Vicharati dhamikasa,* i.e. "the great devout wanders". The southern face of this rock shows prominently Parthian soldiers in their typical attire in the act of hunting while along with other animals here horses are drawn in typical Achaemenian tradition. There are several stupas with dedicatory inscriptions.

The most important part of the "Altar Rock" is the western boulder, which has unique engraving of a scene on a surface facing south. Here, beside three stupas in the middle we have haloed Maitreya on the left, the seated figure of the Buddha without halo in the left middle, the story of *Sibi Jataka* in the right middle, and on the extreme right is another Jataka story representing a sage (probably Buddha) feeding the animals. On the upper part of this surface we have the seated figure of Avalokitesvara on the top and below him two seated figures, both of them haloed, in hot discussion. The inscriptions name them as Avalokitesvara and Manju Sri, the two Bodhisattvas whose followers must have played schismatic role in this part. The other figures are also labelled. And then we also get the unique inscription reading *Vicharati Devadata Sabodhapati,* i.e. "Devadatta, Lord of Knowledge, wanders". Such an inscription of Devadatta, the rival cousin of Buddha, shows the heterogenous tendencies among the Buddhists at this time. We also note the high place given here to Bodhisattva Avalokitesvara. It is for this reason that Buddha is shown without halo.

At another place there is a late figure of Buddha on one face and on another several Buddhas beside the drawing of a monastic structure. At another place there are two noble horses drawn in T'ang style.

From the "Altar Rock" we can now move east and west along the hill and if we climb up a little we can be on the old pilgrim path and see many more carvings on way. Here we have seated Buddhas in typical Gandhara style of 5th century AD. We have triple temples with inscriptions. At one place an elaborate temple is drawn with terraced *sikhara* (spire) decorated with dots. At another place below a stupa Buddha is seated under a pipal tree, the tree enclosing the whole body of Buddha as if in a halo, and from the right side a heavenly personage is approaching in a devotional mood. The whole scene is probably representing the enlightenment of Buddha in a novel style. The inscription gives

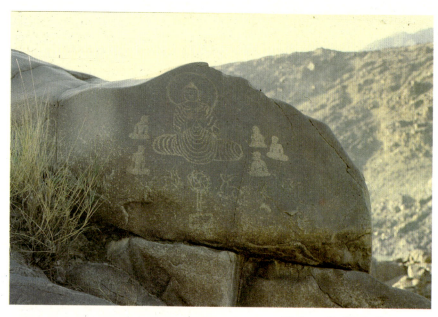

Thalpan: Buddha's first serman.

Thalpan : Parthian hunter with his kill.

the name of the donor as Ranchanavahana. At another place there is a stupa (temple?) with a lion capital on its either side. At still another place there is a long inscription, in late Brahmi, invoking the Bodhisattva Avalokitesvara. It must also be noted that at this late period Brahmin preachers had already penetrated the Thalpan plain. Their inscriptions are found along with the representation of *trisula* (trident) and phallus.

When we go westward from "Altar Rock", we have to climb up to a higher terrace on a pebbly and stony slope until we reach a huge boulder, sufficiently tall for a momentary shelter. The pilgrim path marches on by its side while to the north is the deserted village of Thakot, the dry soil of which now hangs along the hill slope. The *maidan* (plain) to the west shows the scatter of boulders that have been rolled down from the hill top. Most of them have been blackened through climatic action. These scattered boulders right upto the edge of the Indus river bank have preserved the records of man from prehistoric time right upto 19th century, when the graves of two martyrs recall the events of Dogra invasion. These graves are locally called *Ziarats*. As we slowly march towards them to pay our respects, our eyes fall on one or other boulder and we read the inscriptions in Kharoshthi or Brahmi and at the farthest end two Sogdian inscriptions in two different places. Several stupas are seen. Mounted horsemen display their own

Thalpan : Buddha in Gandhara style.

symbols. Temples along with label inscriptions come on our way. But of greatest importance is a series of prehistoric carvings that are seen between two *Ziarats*. It is near the first *Ziarat* that a Central Asian prince in his typical attire of Samarkand is seen worshipping a stupa while nearby is another Central Asian man standing beside a tall lamp.

The prehistoric carving shows several scenes of hunting, snake biting, palm and foot impressions, ibexes and markhors, domestic dog and other animals, fetish objects, raft carried by men for river crossing, men in dancing mood, men holding hand in hand, man fighting with snake and several other human acts. One typical scene of a man is notable where he is being bitten by two snakes but he has lifted up one child and scared away another child. One group hunting scene is remarkable, in which men armed with bows and arrows or simply stones in their hands are trying to hit an ibex. Another shows a hunter with horns on his head piercing the arrow into the body of an animal. In another place a beautiful bull is drawn with a man facing him. Still another place shows a horse drawn in an archaic style.

There are two deities shown. One is a simple drawing of a human with outstretched hands, and feet, which are apart, are tied. This is a poor copy of the giant man seen on the left bank of the Indus river at the Deva site. The second

Thalpan : Parthian hunter and stupas.

figure is seen on a western face of a rock, the other side of which shows human and palm and foot impressions. In the morning light it is very difficult to see it. It is an anthropomorphic deity represented in geometric lines. The body is formed by a square with brisling hair on top. The hands are at an incline with five fingers shown clearly and a snake at the left arm. The two legs are joined and taper down to a point with feet drawn outwardly in a fashion suggesting the form of a boat. The art style is derived from the terracotta figurines of the 1st and second millennium B.C. but the concept here is entirely different. Could it be a snake-god or a river-god of the prehistoric man? Whatever may be the identification, that makes a great addition to our knowledge of the religious idea of the prehistoric people who must have lived here on either side of the Indus river in the first few millennia before the Christian era. The prehistoric carving presents a social life in which hunting of the animals dominated economic life. Socially they lived in groups with women and children and enjoyed dancing and group life. They wore animal horns on their heads and probably also animal skin on their body. Their best companion was dog and their greatest fear was snake. Although they were primarily hunters, yet their life style was much advanced from the palaeolithic concepts. Their deities and fetish objects as well as their art style make them contemporary with other neolithic people.

Thalpan : Buddha in Gandhara style.

As we witness the remnants of the past on one or the other boulder over the plain, our journey becomes more and more difficult because nature has not been kind to this dry plain. Far up in the distance we see the only green patch near a water spring, otherwise the area is dry with many dry rivulets dissecting the plain with their torrential flow during occasional floods. it is these dry channels which make our journey very difficult. We have to cross several *das* on our way. The adventure becomes hazarduous and tiresome. But we have the satisfaction of seeing more and more as we move ahead. It is this passion of adventure that keeps us marching until we reach Khomar, actually two Khomars, where the carvings fade away. We may see some later caves used by shepherds even today. Onward the journey leads to Darbati and to Hodur where life is recreated on stones as we have seen earlier. The intermediate space is barren probably because there was no hunt available. However, the pilgrim path, over which we have trekked, has given us a cross-section of human history engraved on rocks and stones. They are open treasure records of the past of man to show us a type of life that was possible on the upper Indus course beyond the Himalaya, a life that is dead and gone but can still be visualized from the silent town of Chilas just at the foot of Nanga Parvat (Dyamar).

Thalpan : Nestorian Cross.

From Chilas to Gilgit

Beyond Thalpan and Thak *nala* the carvings disappear completely along KKH probably because this was not the old route. Higher up at the old village of Gini, far to the south, carvings are reported. Not until we reach Gauharabad, on the right bank of the Indus river, we have hardly anything of old to see on way. There are open plains, new village developments, new shops but all these came in recent years. The British farm development can be seen at a height at Bonar Similarly new agricultural experiment can be noted at Gonar. But it is only at Gauharabad that we get an old fort of the mediaeval period and in its vicinity there are carvings of mounted horsemen and other animals. From the height of Gauharabad we have a beautiful view of Nanga Parvat (Dyamar) far to the south of KKH. Further ahead comes the Raikot bridge on the Indus, where we cross the river and then onward we drive along the right bank of the river. Barren, dry and rocky hills, sometimes overlain with soily deposits, can be seen on way. The Indus river is actually rounding the Nanga Parvat (Dyamar) on the south and skirting the Karakorum range on the north. This is the most featureless countryside through which we drive until we reach the Sai valley near Janglot. It is from the side of Janglot that we have another marvellous view of Nanga Parvat (Dyamar), particularly in the morning hours when the sun rays bounce upon the snow-capped peak. One can witness a wonderful communion between the solar rays and the snowy rise of the peak.

Gilgit : (Kunodas) Nestorian Cross.

Nanga Parvat and Indus River.

Sai valley is the western-most boundary line of Gilgit region proper. The valley maintained its old little kingdom in the past. There is a direct access along the Sai *nala,* across a high pass, over to Khinnar valley and to Thalpan and Chilas but this is not open during winter. It is probably this route that was followed by the Chinese pilgrim Hiuen Tsang to reach the country of Bolor, the old name of Gilgit kingdom, from Ta-lilo, the Chilas region. Janglot on KKH is a newly growing settlement. The old Janglot is further removed to the north about a mile away, beyond which spreads the beautiful green valley named after the Sai river, which actually drains the water of many other rivulets. It is from inside the valley near the village of Damot that one can go towards Chilas if we follow one rivulet and can proceed to Gilgit if we follow another rivulet. From KKH if one looks towards the hill top over the Sai n*ala,* one can have a distant view of a mediaeval fortified place but for a better view one has to go to the old village of Janglot and beyond to Damot, which provides a beautiful perspective of the entire valley. About five miles away from new Janglot Gilgit river meets the Indus, which comes from the direction of Skardu, the district headquarter of Baltistan. Damot is the old village in the Sai valley. The present village stands just on the bank of the nala but the old fortified town was further away on the hill top to the west. There are actually two fortified places, built one after the other, the northern and the southem settlements. It is the southern settlement that is visible from KKH. But the norhtern part is much older and more important. To the extreme north there is a promontory of the hillock, on which a small castle was originally built. Sometime during the mediaeval period this was completely burnt and destroyed. In between the blocks of stones that went to make the walls of the castle ashes and charcoal are seen in several places. This castle must have served as a watch tower as it commands a good view of the entire fertile Sai valley. At the foot of this hillock there is a plain high ground, now turned into fields. At one place a sculptured stone statue is preserved in situ underground. It is a standing Buddhist figure. Unfortunately the statue is much defaced because the local people throw stones at it. Hence this has been deliberately kept inside the earth. The style of the sculpture appears to be of the same type as the one preserved at Gilgit (Kargah Buddha).

Opposite Sai valley is the plain of Boonji on the left bank of the Indus river just at the point where it turns abruptly to the south after Gilgit river meets it. Boonji lies at the foot of the southern hill and gives access to the extensive Astor valley, the old route to Kashmir It marks the eastern limit of Nanga Parvat (Dyamar) In Astor valley there are some beautiful lakes, the most famous being Rama lake, wherefrom the best view of Nanga Parvat (Dyamar), can be had Major Biddulph says about old Boonji:

"This was at one time a flourishing settlement, and is said to have contained eight forts, which would represent a population of between 2000 and 3000 souls Its prosperity began to decline under the influence of the wars undertaken at the beginning of the present (19th) century by the rulers of Yasin and Chitral, which finally led to the Sikh occupation of Gilgit In 1841 Boonji only contained 200 houses, and it was then finally ruined by the disastrous floods, of which Mr. Drew gives so interesting and able an explanation. The watercourses, on which the prosperity of such alluvial spots entirely depends, were swept away."

As we proceed towards Indus Gilgit confluence, we get a better view of the two rivers, one coming from the north and another coming from south-east, along which we can see the road leading towards Skardu after rounding the hill right in front. Just before the confluence, immediately on the right side of KKH, there are two big boulders, which have carvings on them. On boulder No. 1, we see, on the right, a horseman and below him two markhors. On the left, we have one ibex and a markhor, and below them two horsemen, and still below two horsemen and a *svastika*. The other boulder has a Brahmi inscription reading *Sri Chayana (?) senasya*. On the other side of this rock there are several horsemen, ibexes and markhors, on the top a row of horsemen and on the other side a repetition of the same.

About three km. from this place is the Alam bridge (now called Farhad bridge) on the Gilgit river, along which KKH now runs. KKH gives a by-road to this bridge which ultimately becomes the Skardu road. If we follow this road about a mile and a half, we reach a point just before the road turns round the hill. This is just opposite the carved boulders seen on the other side of the Gilgit river. Here right on the riverside we find a yellow rock outcrop, which contains several inscriptions and carvings, so well described by the French Professor G. Fussman. One boulder shows a stupa of an entirely different type on the top. This type is seen in the Skardu area. On the left is a horseman facing left, and below an ibex facing right. On the right other horsemen are seen and below them two ibexes. Another boulder has Brahmi inscription on the left and on the right a circle and a trident and two lines of Kharoshthi. Other boulders show ibexes along with compartmented squares and circles with dots within of a type already known from Chilas region. Thus these late carvings have a direct relationship with those seen in the Chilas area. On the other hand one rock has a beautiful carving of an ibex and another of a bull, both having curved horns, in an entirely new style. The inscriptions make an interesting study as they continue for some centuries in Kharoshthi and Brahmi. There is one Tibetan inscription also. They relate to Buddhism, Hindu Saivism or Vaishnavism or some local cults. In one Kharoshthi inscription the word Daradaraya (prince of Daradas) has been read.

Gilgit

Gilgit is an old name derived from the original Girigitta that appears in the Hatun rock inscription of seventh century A.D. As we move northward along KKH on the right side of Gilgit river, we come to the point where Hunza river joins Gilgit river, about six miles from Gilgit city proper. Soon after the confluence there is a bridge over the Gilgit river. Here KKH turns on this bridge and bids good-bye to the Gilgit road. KKH now goes to the next village of Danyor and onward to Hunza. The confluence of the two rivers at Danyor provides other interesting sites for study. At Danyor itself, in a private house of Habib Mazhar, son of Ali Madad, there is a huge rock, partly broken towards the upper end, measuring 13' long and 17" wide, containing long Sanskrit inscription in the late Brahmi character of 8th century A.D. running into five lines. The inscription belongs to the same line of rulers who are mentioned in Hatun inscription, and gives all the royal titles of *Patola shahi Shahanushahi* and *Parama-bhattaraka* to the ruler of *Vikrarnaditya* family, whose name is *Jayamangala Vikramaditya Nandi*. The two other descendants of the ruler are also named. The inscription was written by the prince *(Kumaramatya)*. It speaks

Nanga Parvat from Hodur

of the conquest by the local ruler, probably implying the overthrow of the raid of the Tibetans;

We leave the site of the inscription and come back to KKH and proceed towards Dah *nala,* which joins the Hunza river, we come to another site of rock carvings just before their confluence. There are two big boulders on the left bank of Dah *nala* and one small carved boulder on way. A big boulder is divided into two parts by a vertical, each part can be studied into three sections. The lowest section of the left part shows three markhors with twisted horns. The second section shows seven ibexes with one man standing on right holding bow and arrow. The third section shows only three ibexes. On the second part the second section has three markhors, numerous ibexes with horns curved back and four to five horse-riders running roughshod in their midst. This section has also two markhors. The lowest section has only one markhor. In the third section the ibexes have long curved horns while the next section shows ibexes with angular curved horns. On the western side of this rock there is only one markhor and twelve ibexes.

When we cross the Hunza river by a narrow bridge from Danyor, we come to the site of Kunodas, not far from the newly built Government College of Gilgit. There is also another approach to this site from the airport road through another bridge that leads from Gilgit city to the College. About hundred yards from the College there is a pile of big boulders lying at random on a pebbly surface on the bank of the river. The stones are of varying sizes. At one place a big boulder is placed on small stones in such a fashion that it makes a little shelter. At another place three big boulders are standing in an order suggesting some sort of a ritual. Several boulders have animal carvings of different periods. The oldest carvings show only ibexes and markhors. Later carvings include horses and horsemen. Of this period some hunters are also seen. Still later some wheels and other symbols were introduced. One can also recognise modern carvings. On one rock, beside animal carvings, we have a Nestorian Christian cross. It seems that later this site was used for cremation by the Hindus.

The third important site in Gilgit is seen in the Kargah valley. This valley lies about seven miles away from Gilgit towards Punyal. A small stream called Shukugah joins this Kargah stream. The Shukugah divides the hill in front into two. On the western face of this hill is seen the standing figure of Buddha in *abhaya* (fearlessness) pose. Originally it was within a niche, the holes of which are still preserved around the figure. The Buddha is sculptured and is in Tibetan style as we also find at Satpara lake near Skardu. On the top of this hill stray masonry construction are seen from far. It is reported that on the other side of the

Prof. K. Jettmar before Nanga Parvat.

Gilgit : (Kunodas) Rock carving.

hill there is a large and long cave and many other constructions. Down below is the so-called Phid-das stupa, whlch has prominent round structure built of rough stones laid in mud mortar. It occupies a high natural hillock, to which access is provided by a stairway on the north. At different stages some later masonry wall was constructed in order to strengthen the high stupa tower. At several places ash and charcoal are seen, suggesting that towards the end the whole thing was burnt. From this top a beautiful view of the Gilgit river and the whole of Gilgit valley can be had. At the flat ground below four square rooms are still existing. These were later formed part of Buddhist monastery. It is from the second room that Gilgit manuscript was discovered. Much later in history this entire area, called today as Napursa, supported an old habitation and one corner of which was used as a citadel of the local ruler. The top of the stupa, which shows later masonry construction, may have been used as a defensive post. It is from this top that a British made rifle bullet case was recovered. Here potsherds are scattered all over the place. They are mainly of two varieties. A later coarse red pottery of modern time and earlier finely polished red pottery.

If we proceed inside Kargah valley, we see the two power houses which supply power to the city. But the most important is a big cave at some great height. It is about sixty feet wide and more than three hundred feet deep. The cave appears to have been finished by human hand. Inside there is a water spring. The interior housed a whole village, the ruined walls of which are still preserved. A footpath has been cut along the rock at that height leading into the village from the further side of the Kargah valley and then it goes towards Kargah Buddha.

When we come back to Punyal road and proceed towards Shingel, we meet several carvings of animals and horsemen, ruined stupa structure at Hanzel, multiple burial on hill top near Bubur and also at Gopis, several inscribed boulders near the fishery at Gopis, a conical sculptured stone piece showing sculptures on three faces in a field at Bubur, and onward to different valley of Ishkomen, Yassin and across the Shandul pass to Chitral.

Nestorian Cross.

Gilgit : (Kargah) Buddha.

From Gilgit to Hunza

From Gilgit we go to Danyor and drive along KKH. Just before the village of Jutial we find, on our right, several blackened granitic boulders. Some of them have animal carvings on them mostly ibexes. These boulders are spread out to some distance. On the other side of the Hunza river is Nomal village. The old Hunza road can be seen on that side of the river. It leads to the high plateau of Naltar - a beautiful pasture land and picnic spot, where animals wander about freely in their natural setting.

Further ahead we come to a petrol pump but just before that is the famous village of Chhalt on the right bank of Hunza river. A bridge takes us to that village. In Chhalt Payin, immediately at the entrance of the village, there are two big boulders. One on the right side of the road has an ibex and stupa carved on it. Onward we go to Chhalt Bala and from there to Sonikot, situated on the bank of Garamsai *nala*. Here we see big boulders. The biggest squarish boulder, facing north-east, has carving on it. We see two stupas in the middle standing on terraces, having dome and trident-ending finial. They are flanked by an ibex. Below more markhors are seen.

We come back to KKH and pass by the new settlement of Sikandarabad. At Gulmat Bala there is a big *Ziarat*. It is from this village that the climbers start for Rakaposhi—a picturesque glacier that dominates all the way to Karimabad, the headquarter of Hunza. Chhalt and Sikandarabad are actually in Nagir tehsil and from here onward we are passing through both the areas. Green fields of both the tehsils meet occasionally our eyes and they are seen in terraces right upto the top of the hills. These dangerous fields are the work of the local people. In between one can see some old villages still preserving the old style of village planning and house construction. It is only at the foot of Karimabad that we find the two rivers Hunza and Nagir meeting. The road to Karimabad takes off from KKH at Aliabad, where we have tent accommodation. Karimabad rises up on the right side of Hunza river. The town spreads like a green overgrowth of houses and fields in terraces interspersed with poplar and fruit trees. The new palace of the Mir of Hunza is on the right. The old Baltit fort is on the left. Still further is the older fort of Altit built in the typical local style of wooden architecture. Right at the bottom is the old village of Ganesh and beyond is the bridge on Hunza river that takes to the Sacred Rock of Hunza on the side of KKH.

Sacred rock of Hunza

The Sacred Rock of Hunza stands boldly in the middle of a small bowl-like valley and is washed on its northern side by the gurgling Hunza river that breaks through a narrow gorge on the east to force itself into this valley. The river splashes against the Sacred Rock and gradually bends its way on its northern side, thus separating the Rock from the ruined ancient habitation high up on its northern bank, now remembered by the surviving Altit fort and many dilapidated field terraces, poplar trees and bushes that abundantly hang on the slopes, crevices and old pathways of the eroded elevation on the opposite hill. The river has eaten up the open plain ground on the eastern front of the Sacred Rock, thus exposing the earlier gravel and clay deposits and by the way revealing its earlier higher bed in the remote past. It was then that the river erosion washed away the roughness of the Sacred Rock and scooped several smooth niche-like formations. The process is still going on at a lower level. These niches of the higher level were used by the ancient man for his own creation. It is natural that the eastern front of the Sacred Rock, that has been cleanly washed and smoothed by the river currents, and that faces the rising sun, should have been the earliest place for human activity.

Hunza : Altit Fort beside Hunza river.

Today this frontage is spoiled by the fall of the rocks from above. They have made a mess of this side and concealed probably some of the carvings that reach down the present rough ground. These rocks certainly fell down much later as the lower portion of some of them still bear under their lower side writings of old. Moreover the bare eastern face higher up shows the rough scars from where these rocks have parted company. Nature and later blasting for rubies by man have done further damages to the Sacred Rock and left cracks and loose stones. Still the Sacred Rock has stood adamantly through the ravages of time and maintained the carvings and writings of men to tell us about the long forgotten history of the place and of the pathway along which man travelled from China to Gandhara. The new Karakorum Highway that runs along its southern front has now opened up new prospects of travel and led to the discovery of this monument of world importance that remained hidden for centuries from the eyes of the people. However, it was known to the local people as Haldeikish, i.e. the place of the male ibexes. It is these ibex carvings that predominate the entire rock surface as seen from the.Highway. The carvings recall the eternal local tradition of the ceremony of ibex hunting, known as *thuma saling* in the local language.

The river side of the Sacred rock has been left free to nature as it is very steep down to the river except occasional visits to the newly made niches, where we can see a few animal carvings and also a series of tridents drawn by man.

Hunza : Altit Fort beside Hunza river.

Hunza Roak : Kushana Man.

However, it is the eastern front that engaged the attention of man from remote past. Further extension higher up was made both on the river side and on the road side to provide space for new activities of man. The roadside shows the remnants of a natural cavern higher up on the third stage, to which approach was made by a sloping ramp-like formation of the rock surface right from the western front and also to the river side, thus making the upper space available to man for writing.

Eastern front shows, on its left, a small niche-like formation, where ibexes of different periods occupy the main lower space. To the left is definitely older carving of jumping ibexes, now very dim, before another ibex, which has dotted horns and is walking to right. It is immediately below this ibex that a later carving of a standing man to front in typical Kushana dress of long robe, peaked cap, left hand at the waist and right extended slightly upward—a figure that exactly corresponds with the type of imperial Kushana personage on the coins from the time of Wima Kadphises onward. To his left and right are two ibexes with angular bent horns walking towards him. A very indistinct elephant, with upturned trunk in salutation, also appears on his left. This imperial portrait of the

Hunza : Bhitan Dance.

Kushana emperor is further highlighted by a marginal Kharoshthi inscription on the top, which reveals the name of the first Kushana emperor in these words: *Dramika Maharaja Dunamanta Kadhatphisa,* i.e. "the most devout, the great king, steadfast, Kadphises". The inscription has some thing to do with the figure below. However, the evidence proves that this area was withing the. authority of the Kushana kings. Below this inscription is the name of the govemor,, *Kshattapa Nuusakha-putra Dhoihola,* who makes a donation. Below this a peculiar symbol, looking a phallus on a pedestal. Before it a man stands in defiance.

The central niche of the easten front is the biggest but is now spoiled by cracks and rock falls. Its floor is full of debris. On its right curve the Kharoshthi inscriptions have become dim but one of them gives the name of *Samghamitra.* On its left top is now preserved a Kharoshthi inscription dated 69 (i.e. 78 + 69 = A.D. 147), written in a box-like character, and speaking of the Kshatrapa *Sudihakhu* when Revadamitra perfomred the ceremony of his father Revada. On its top is seen a symbol, which appears like a *svastika,* but actually it is a cryptic Buddhist symbol reading *Dharmasa.*

To the right of this central niche are smaller niches. At the bottom are some memorable scenes and inscriptions. On the right hand side the two rows of humans in different dancing poses with their hands flung in different postures while to their left, in the first row, are two animals facing left. Above this is a single line of Kharoshthi inscription speaking of the gift to a monastery by *Khushana Devaputra Maharaja Kanishka.* Still above is a dated inscription of the reign of Huvishka when *Samghamitra* does something. To the left of all this is a graphic hunting scene, where men armed with bows and arrows chase the running animals while a beautiful horse is being led by a man above and a goat is standing in his stupid simplicity down. The name *Maharaya Huvishka is* again repeated on the left top above two stylised symbols of a phallus and a tree.

While these older Kharoshthi inscriptions speak of human devotion to Buddhism, later dated inscriptions in Gupta Brahmi script narrate a different story. They talk of the capture of *Siha, Sihavarma, Sihodharavarma, Kashyapa, Mayura* and his son in the years 103 and 104, obviously in Gupta era, i.e. 319 + 103 = A.D.422 and 319 + 104 = A.D. 423. On the right top the new ruler assumes the title of *Kshema Sri Nripendra* while in the central niche the name of *Chandra Sri Deva or Soma Sri Deva* occurs. Who is this ruler? Wherefrom did he come? The history is not clear on this face until we turn to the roadside where there is a jumble of inscriptions one above the other with later animal carvings

Hunza Roack : Kushana Emperor Wima Kedphises

Hunza : Sacred Rock and K.K.H.

defacing some of them in several niches at several levels. In this jumble one can catch several dates in Kharoshthi, all falling within the reign of the Kushana emperor Vasudeva. It is in this jumble that we get a clean Gupta writing of Mitradeva, who established here an institution of charity.

At the second stage on the right hand side of a corner stone we read the name *Vikramadi (tya)* in the Gupta character. And then to the left above the Kharoshthi inscriptions on a prominent place is written in Gupta Brahmi:

Sam.... Sri Vikramaditya Jayati Sri Chandra i.e. "In the year.... the glorious Vikramaditya Sri Chandra conquers." The last word is written in a very florid style, probably copying a signature. This may be contrasted from the cursive writing seen in the underside of the top little niche over the central niche on the eastern part.

While these inscriptions speak of the change of royalties and dynasties, the eternal story of the ibex dominates over all of them. They are seen everywhere with their long curved horns, or with crossed bodies, but the horse, in its simple outline, is very realistic, while a standing man on horseback exhibits his audacity and bravery and at the same time it recalls similar horseriders from the region of Chilas. It seems that ultimately they became dominant in this part of the world. If

Hunza : King's head and late Brahmi inscription..

this is correct, these people must have moved into this direction and established their authority all over the Northern areas of Pakistan.

The rows of ibexes on the left bottom lead us on to a spot where a remarkable hunting scene is depicted. While a horseman on the left is stopping the long curved horned ibexes, another man, armed with bows and arrows on the right, is shooting at the animals. There is a wild confusion among the animals depicted by unrecognisable signs and lines.

We pass on to the second stage where a lone ibex facing right catches our attention. Above is a fourline inscription in Sogdian, which, as read by Dr. DN. Mackenzie, means *Wishta(sp) son of Athffiy(a) (of) Tashar* f?). To its top right is an inscription in Gupta Brahmi. which reads.

Harishena iha dharma chakam pratishthita
i.e "Harishena established here (Buddhist) wheel of law."

Several representations of ibexes lead us on to the almost end of this Rock No. I but this last part has some more stories to tell. A flat area, immediately left of the place where the old sloping ramp started, has a small baby animal facing

Hunza : Another head and bird.

right with an inscription in Brahmi to its front in two lines again speaking of *"Harish (ena) here"* and below it another Brahmi inscription written across the horns of a grown-up ibex. The inscription gives the name of Sri Chandra.

However, the most remarkable place is a series of end niches, displaying a multiplicity of ibexes of different periods in different styles as if they are wandering over the bare hill. There is a bigger central niche in the middle, flanked by smaller niches on right and left. The central niche has, on its right side, carvings in the upper part as well as in the lower part. The upper part has, besides ibexes, the typical Buddhist cryptic symbol derived from *Svastika*. In the lower part the ibexes have short horns, except one facing right. On the left hand side of this niche some of the ibexes have solid bodies others have extremely curved horns with a dot in the middle. In between are smaller ibexes, probably babies. These ibexes have on their top a Brahmi inscription of Harishena giving a date. The left hand side niche has at the bottom two solid big ibexes and other smaller ones. Here comes the end of the 1st Rock on the roadside.

If we turn now to the river side of Rock No.1, we find it sloping in an undulating fashion. The falling away of the upper portion of the rock has made a mess of the whole area. This river face can be divided into three major parts,

Hunza Rock : Chinese inscription.

termed here alcoves. They are numbered alcove No.1 on the top, alcove No.2 at the bottom and alcove No. 3 in the middle.

Alcove No. 1 can be subdivided into five sub-divisions:

(a) Right curve with a Kharoshthi inscription reading *Bhikhumitra da (na)*, i.e. "Gift of Bhikumitra".

(b) The flat middle part has three sections divided by two longitudinal cracks. The right part has a Brahmi inscription reading *(sam) 100 3 (?) Simha-samprapta*

Kshema Sri Nripendra

i.e. "In the year 103 (?), Lion(quality)-attained Kshema Sri Nripendra"

(c) The central part has another Brahmi inscription reading: *Simha-varma-samprapta*, i.e. "Simhavarma attained".

(d) The western part has Kharoshthi inscriptions reading: *Dhaorana putra dana*, i.e. "gift of the son of Dhaorana". And another inscription reading: *Samgha, Dharma and Buddha*.

(e) The left curve has two Kharoshthi inscriptions reading.

(i) *Dhathu mata pitu puhae.*"The relic, for the merit of mother and father."

(ii) *Samghamitra (putra) Kshatrapa Budhasena Sabatu.*

i.e. "May the governor Budhasena, son of Samghamitra live." There are also three Brahmi inscriptions on the left side. One of them gives the name of Mayuraputra Harikala, and another speaks of the merit of Sarvastivadi Buddhist sect.

Rock No. II

There is an abrupt old break and then the second rock suddenly rises, showing several weatherings on its face and fall of rocks from top. One rock, in front, now broken into two, has some symbols including *svastika,* a stupa and Brahmi inscription of *Sri Nripendra* in Gupta character. Another big rock to the left has some cursive inscriptions and symbols. The main rock then suddenly loses its height and there are several rock falls to the front, three of which are big boulders. The right hand side, which faces the road, has some important things to reveal with two heads represented on them. Further ahead a little rock face on the left shows some animals. Then lone ibexes facing left lead one to a remarkable small niche facing the road. Other ibexes on the left side of the niche also turn their face towards the niche as if all the animals point to the importance of the niche. Here within the niche is a late Brahmi inscription of 8th-9th century A.D. The inscription for the first time gives the tribal name *Trakha*, probably referring to the Trakhan dynasty who ruled over Gilgit and Hunza after the overthrow of the Patola Shahis and started the mediaeved history of the region. The inscription is traslated thus:

"Lion of the Trakha (Turk) qualities, Ramudasa, the king, (is) victorious, hail, hail, to the umbrella and fly-whisp of the civilised dynasty of gods (who has) crossed from peak to peak."

The animals depicted on the left side of the niche have semi circular horns with a big circle within the curve. As we proceed ahead, we meet some remarkable horse-riders. A further series of ibexes lead us ahead. Some of these

Sust Carving.

have crossed bodies, some have fat body shown in outline, and some have solid filled in bodies. Then we come to a horse–rider leading the animals to right. To its front another small rock fall gives the name of *Buddhadasa* written in Brahmi character. And finally we come to the end niche of this rock where several ibexes are carved.

The second rock has a remarkable Chinese inscription written from top to bottom, speaking of a Chinese ambassador coming from the court of Ta-Wei dynasty. The inscription is translated thus:

"Gu Wei-Long, envoy of great Wei is despatched to Mi-mi now."

Another ambassador by the name of Sung-Yun came in in about 520 A.D. to the court of Yetha from China. To the left of this inscription are two stupas, each one on a high terrace, and to the right is a Brahmi inscription giving the name of Harishena. On the right of the stupa there is another Brahmi inscription reading *Sri Chandradevasya*. And finally we come to the remarkable big boulder, which shows on the top a human head, looking left, having sharp nose, round head, long eyes and two pigtails behind. His forehead is flush with the nose. His name is written across in Brahmi, *reading Sra Hranka Sri Ya(ddha Sim(ha)*. This may be the name of governor, or his title. Below this head is a jumble of inscription. written over earlier drawing of animals. Some inscriptions are on earlier writing. Among them we read the older names of Buddharakshita and Rudradasa but new names like Bhadra Vishnu Chichi Savro are entirely new. On the side facing west of this rock we have a small bird and another head of a different kind with protruding chin.

Rock III is a low rock with sparse ibexes only in one place. This rock gradually slopes down towards the north and ends in rubbles and pebbles, probbaly the work of rubi miners.

Rock No. IV

There are some rubbles Iying in the opening between the third and the fourth rocks. This Rock IV suddenly rises high almost to the same height as the top of the second rock. This height goes on in an undulating fashion to the end when it suddenly breaks off. On the roaside there was originally a thick deposit of pebbles and gravels, the top of which was the working floor of the people who made the carvings on this rock. Now the deposit has been cut through by the road builders. The onginal surface is still preserved on the right side of the Highway. Further ahead is a thick clayey deposit, part of which has been used as graveyard by the people of Ganesh. This alternate deposit of pebble stratum and clay against the western height of the tertiary hill speaks of the earlier geological phase. There is no cultural material so far found here. The erosion of these deposits from the western face of Rock No. lV has exposed the original rock surface which was free for human activity. Hence all the drawings were made much later than these deposits.

The rock has many new things to tell. There is only one Brahmi inscription in the Gupta writing of 5th century A.D., and another inscription in cursive writing. The rest show humans, animals and some symbols. Except one human individual, who is in typical Kushana dress, all others are very crude but they now show five fingers in their hands. Horses are depicted in large number, some of which have wheels attached to the lege. There is one clear deep niche in this rock while other drawings occupy flat surfaces.

Beginning from the side facing south, we get a small group of ibexes at the bottom right, which are all deeply engraved. On their top is a man, with his hands

Raka Poshi Glacier

akimbo, standing in a fashion as if in a talking mood with an ill-drawn animal to his front. Passing on to left, we get a man holding in his hand a string tied to a goat, which is obviously being drawn. Below this scene is the Brahmi legend *Vijaya Vahi* ("conquest of Vahi"), a deity also seen at Chilas. To its bottom left there is another scene in three rows, the middle row being very dim. Here we have, in the first row, four humans, each alternating with an ibex facing him, in the second row two humans and in the third three. The humans have their hands in different poses and the animals also seem to be active, as if all of them are in some joint activity, probably in dancing activity.

After passing a few more carved animals on way, we come directly to the deep niche. The central object of attraction in this niche is an open dagger placed vertically down into a medley of ibexes. The dagger has parallel lines horizontally across its blade and a dot with short T-shaped handle—a type which is very old. To its right is another dagger with an ibex in between. To its right again are two hanging zigzag ropes. In two other places there is a repetition of this motif. On the left side of the niche the main attraction is a peculiar horseman, riding a horse having a bushy tail and wheeled legs. The man is holding bridle in his left hand and the right probably holding a bow. To his front are numerous ibexes but in the middle are two vertically hanging zigzag ropes. Down below is another carved human. On the outside face of the niche at the bottom there is a horse, with its body shown by double line. To its top left is a ferocious ibex with its horns bent in a fighting mood.

Next we come to another scene where we see a group of engraved ibexes at the bottom and above four horsemen with a whip in hand on running horse. One man is standing on ground in the middle with male ibexes above, on right and left. One ibex has filled-in thick body while another has crossed body. On the top of this is another group of ibexes with a tree in the middle. Still above is another group of ibexes with a human showing his five fingers in each hand. After passing through more animals we come to a small shallow niche, having two humans with five-fingered hands, each before two ibexes, as if they are in a joint activity. To its left is again a rope hanging from a hood and ending in a cross, three ends of which have hooks.

Then we come to a deeper niche, left side of which shows carved and engraved ibexes alongwith a cursive writing. Some older drawings are very faint but the new ones show thick body. On one place there is a spider. More horsemen and ibexes follow on the left. Then come six successive small niches, each having its own peculiarity. In the first niche we have a circle, subdivided

Yak at khunjrab

into four segments, each having a dot. There is also a spider on the right. In the second niche, besides the animals and humans, we have rope design, a circle with semi-circles at the inner arch, an ibex with three circles within the curve of its horns. Some more hunting scenes follow. Between the fourth and fifth niche humans are standing with outstretched hands having five fingers each. There is also a solar symbol.

As we proceed towards the left, deep engravings are not seen at all. But horsemen and ibexes continue in shallow technique. At one place three ibexes are in a single file, behind which follow smaller bodies. More ibexes follow and lead us on to the lowest flat surface where we see only four ibexes looking right towards a man standing to front with a horseman before him. Both the man and horseman are drawn in a different hand and are older than the ibexes. The man is putting on typical Kushana dress. His both hands are at the waist. His head is dim but seems to have an orb around the head. The horseman is standing before him as if to give a message. The figure is no doubt royal and the message is given directly to him.

Thereafter no drawings are seen and the rock abruptly slopes down to the ground level.

As we walk back from the end of the rock on the right side of the road, we come to a pile of blackened boulders. On two of them are carvings. One shows a single ibex and another has a design probably signifying a load on an animal, topped over by a water vessel. One rock has a Brahmi inscription, reading *pratishthita iha shamano,* i.e. "the monk is established here". Another boulder has a bigger inscription facing the road, reading:

> *Sampasarasya sisya nama*
> *Vasukirti Sramano*
> ie. *"The monk, named Vasukirti, disciple of Sampasara."*

On an isolated rock further away to the south in front of the two caves recently dug by the Chinese road builders, we have an isolated rock. At its bottom, on the side facing the hill, we have two rows of ibexes. One of them has a dot between the curve of the horns.

There are also isolated rocks further away to the east on the left side of the road. Not far from the helipad, right at the bottom of the Highway we see a traveller riding a horse and on its upper side two ibexes are carved. Among other carved boulders, the most important is a rock shelter just near the river bank. On the side facing the road we have several ibexes and below a man on horseback. The actual shelter is on the northern side. The side boulders which make up the shelter show ibexes and more of them are seen on the floor. The shelter has also Brahmi inscriptions on the outside as well as inside. On the left the inscription reads *"Sri Charanasya"* and on the extreme left it reads *Siha samprapta Chandra Sri Deva Vikramaditya,* i.e. "Chandra Sri Deva Vikramaditya obtained (i.e. conquered).... Siha." Another inscription reads *Dharmapriya...Buddha (Bhikshu),* i.e. "The Buddhist monk Dharmapriya (Beloved of Dharma)". Two other inscriptions read *Vijaya* (i.e. victory) and another *Sankarasya,* i.e. "Of *Sankara* (i.e. Siva).

Thus this Sacred Rock of Hunza and some isolated boulders trace the history of this part before the writing began, continued with the conquest of the

Kushanas, followed by writings in cursive character and Sogdian scripts, but later Deva Sri Chandra Vikramaditya established his authority here. This ruler must be a local prince although he bears the same name as the Gupta emperor. He was followed by the inscriptions having a head on top middle. These inscriptions fall in the post-Gupa period. It is at about this time that the old Chinese inscription was written. And finally we come to an inscription which has some Tibetan words, probably of the time of Tibetan conquest in early eight century AD. Still later we get an inscription of the Trakha ruler.

From Hunza to Khunjrab

The Journey beyond Sacred Rock of Hunza is thrilling if thrill can be derived from rugged hills and gleaming glaciers that we pass one after the other. Actually at Karimabad there is the Ultur glacier behind Baltit fort, which leads directly on to Passu glacier. If we follow KKH, we have the Sacred Rock on our left and on our right a road takes off towards Nagir and further to Hispar glacier, beyond which lies Skardu. About twenty km. from the Sacred Rock is the village of Amanabad. Just before this small village big blackened boulders are seen on our right. Two boulders join to make a small shelter with a platform in front.

Road through Khunjrab Pass

About six km. away there is another small village of Sirshkot and two km. beyond is a bridge on Hunza, which takes us to the right bank of the river. Finally we come to the beautiful village of Gulmit, which is 25 miles from Aliabad. The settlement climbs up the hill on our left. Upon the hill slope there is a High School. Going beyond the school we come to a spot where big boulders are standing. One such boulder has a single row of nine ibexes and a Brahmi inscription. The only word preserved is *vijita,* i.e. "conquered". After we leave Gulmit village, we come to a *nala,* where on one boulder to our left we see a row of ibexes facing right. Further ahead is the Borit lake, which burst in the year 1980 and destroyed part of KKH but it is now rebuilt. The lake receives glacial water and is visited by birds during summer. From Gulmit onward we are in Wakhi speaking area: Upto this point in Hunza the language was Burushaski.

As we move ahead KKH takes a round of the village of Hussain where we have the *ziarat* of Shah Talib. About seven miles from Gulmit is the village of Passu on the right bank of Hunza river. We see Batura glacier on our left and Passu glacier in front. Beyond the village there is a rivulet coming from Batura glacier and it is the bridge on that rivulet which is called Batura bridge. But two km. before Passu Yasband *nala* crosses KKH to meet Hunza river on our right. About 100 metre down this *nala* there is a big boulder with carvings. Just at the

Pak-China border at Khunjrab.

Khunjrab Pass.

Visitors at Khunjrab.

confluence there are three more carved boulders. One is lying flat on ground and has several carvings. On the top row are four humans with outstretched hands or hands in other poses. In the second row we have a series of horsemen standing on horseback. In the centre is a big horseman standing on a big horse, probably the leader. Below him another man is slashing the horse. In line with these men are ibexes facing right except one which faces left. Still below are three horsemen. Beyond the village of Passu one big boulder has fallen into the river upside down and hence the carvings are not seen now.

Further we meet the villages of Khaibar and Galapan and then comes the opening of Sust, an important station full of green fields and fruit trees. At the northern end of the village we find two limestone boulders, one on the left side of the road and another on the right side. The place is called Bamaldas. The boulder on the left side of KKH has animals drawn by pecking technique. Facing the road, the carvings show two horses and ten ibexes with long curved horns and also one circle with four segments within, each having a dot. The boulder on the right side of the road has, on top, a standing man, and before him ibexes with fat solid body. Down below are two horsemen, and on the other side several horsemen and ibexes. All these figures are also drawn by pecking technique.

Khunjrab Pass : Hot cup of tea.

It is from this point that we cross the Hunza river and go to Khudabad. From here a jeepable road leads to Chapursan *ziarat*. Fifty miles away is Baba-i-Ghundai and beyond is the Wakhan border. This was the ancient route. But today KKH follows left bank of the Hunza river. Five miles away from Sust is Khor Khumbat, where we have hot water springs. Further ahead is the junction of Belli and Hunza rivers. Belli comes from Mintaka glacier from the side of Misgar and Hunza river from Khunjrab. After Sust, along KKH, we do not get any carving because this is a newly built road, but on the older route carvings have been reported. These carvings of horsemen carry forward the tradition of horseriders as we earlier saw at Chilas.

Twenty two miles away from Belli on KKH is the poor settlement of Dih, where we have a checkpost. Two miles before Dih we cross Hunza river again. There is a plan to build a National Park for wild life starting from the bridge here. Dih *nala* comes from north and joins Hunza river. Here we have a wild life hut, in which there is a rest room. Twenty five km. beyond Dih is Ghoshgal-again an open area— otherwise the road passes through overhanging hills. From Ghoshgal we pass to Cookshal, which has a shepherd's hut. On the right is Cookshal *nala*. On the top is Cookshal glacier and beyond is Shimshal.

From Cookshal we turn left and the road winds up twelve miles towards Khunjrab top. As we near the top, the river Hunza slopes down on our right from a little water spring. On the top the snowcapped hills surround an open area, which makes a big grassy bowl in summer. The Pak-China border, at 15077 feet above sea level, is the great divide. Down the Chinese side is the rivulet Yuttar and about fifty miles away is Tashkurgan. We are now in the most beautiful bowllike valley, which presents a panoramic view all round. On our right, if we are lucky, we may have a glance of Marcopolo sheep at a far distance over hill top.

If we leave KKH and follow Belli river, we can go to Misgar, five miles away. Two miles away from Belli we have a rock on our right with four ibexes carved on it. Just before Misgar there are two caves, one having four round entrances and the other three. Inside the cave forty persons can easily live. Misgar is a beautiful green valley. Six miles away from Misgar is Wadwak. At Dardi, 22 miles away from Misgar, are Arabic inscriptions and footprint. It is on the Disand rivulet that Dardi is located. It is this small river that leads to China and in the past this opened the path.

Now we have reached the point where three borders meet. In the past it was the meeting place of humanity, who moved in one or the other direction in search of human destiny. Today the border separates man from man. Let us hope that some day better understanding prevails and humanity again joins hands here to share its load of knowledge, its heritage and its works of art.